The New Lawyer's Handbook

101 Things They Don't Teach You In Law School

KAREN

D1378033

S...
An I...
NAPERVILLE, ILLINOIS
www.SphinxLegal.com

Copyright © 2009 by Karen Thalacker
Cover and internal design © 2009 by Sourcebooks, Inc.

Sourcebooks and the colophon are registered trademarks of Sourcebooks, Inc.

All rights reserved. No part of this book may be reproduced in any form or by any electronic or mechanical means including information storage and retrieval systems—except in the case of brief quotations embodied in critical articles or reviews—without permission in writing from its publisher, Sourcebooks, Inc.

First Edition: 2009

Published by: **Sphinx Publishing, An Imprint of Sourcebooks, Inc.**
Naperville Office
P.O. Box 4410
Naperville, Illinois 60567–4410
630–961–3900
Fax: 630–961–2168
www.sourcebooks.com
www.SphinxLegal.com

This publication is designed to provide accurate and authoritative information in regard to the subject matter covered. It is sold with the understanding that the publisher is not engaged in rendering legal, accounting, or other professional service. If legal advice or other expert assistance is required, the services of a competent professional person should be sought.
    From a Declaration of Principles Jointly Adopted by a Committee of the American Bar Association and a Committee of Publishers and Associations

This product is not a substitute for legal advice.
Disclaimer required by Texas statutes.

Library of Congress Cataloging-in-Publication Data
Thalacker, Karen.
  The new lawyer's handbook : 101 things they don't teach you in law school / by Karen Thalacker.
      p. cm.
   1. Practice of law—United States. 2. Law—Vocational guidance—United States. I. Title.
   KF300.T48 2009
   340.023'73—dc22
                                2009012755

Printed and bound in the United States of America.

VP — 10 9 8 7 6 5 4 3 2 1

To my teachers, mentors, and colleagues

ACKNOWLEDGMENTS

I want to say a special thank you to my family and friends.

To my parents whose wisdom and kindness have always inspired me. I thank God every day that I am your daughter.

To my brothers and sisters—Fred, Ann, Andy, and Laura—who have supported and encouraged me in my crazy adventures from infancy to today.

In writing this book, special thanks to Andy and Laura who are two of the smartest and nicest attorneys I know.

To my children—Ella, Robby, Andy, and Malcolm—who love their busy mom despite my hectic schedule and who give me strength every day.

And to my husband Pete who is my partner in everything. I couldn't and wouldn't do any of this without him.

CONTENTS

Introduction . . . . **xv**

Section I: Starting Out Right at a Law Firm

1. Get the details of your employment
   agreement in writing. 2

2. Appearances matter 4

3. Have extra essentials at the office 7

4. Work when you are at work 10

5. A to-do list is your constant companion 13

6. The importance of having a good assistant . . . 15

7. When you're an associate, *draft* means *final* . . . 18

8. You don't know everything 21

Section II: Understanding Law Firm Politics

9. When your law office is more like the set
   of *Survivor* 24

10. Avoid having a romantic relationship with
    someone in your office 27

11. Foster a close relationship with someone
    in your office who has your back 30

12. It helps to be a golfer. 32

13. What to do if a colleague is struggling 34

Section III: General Tips for Having a Successful Practice

14. Avoiding legal pet peeves. 38

15. Don't tolerate bad behavior 41

16. Learn to be a better listener and a better
    communicator 43

17. Don't give advice to strangers over the phone . . .46

18. Resist the pressure to take a case you're
    not qualified to take 49

19. Find experienced lawyers you can talk to 51

20. Don't procrastinate 53

21. What to do when opposing counsel is a jerk. . 55

22. You can always be a jerk later. 58

23. Think twice before accusing someone of an
    ethical violation 60

Section IV: The Business of Practicing Law

24. Be as involved as possible in your
    law firm's finances....................... 64

25. The importance of a good filing system 67

26. Earning a living as a lawyer is a tough buck .. 70

27. How to build your practice 73

28. Treat your client like a customer 75

29. Get the money up front................. 79

30. How to close a case.................... 82

31. Never let your malpractice insurance lapse ... 84

32. Keep up with your billable hours.......... 86

33. Legal research isn't free anymore 90

34. Disaster planning...................... 93

Section V: Becoming Comfortable with Technology

35. Stay on top of technology but don't
    be a slave to it......................... 98

36. Know how to operate the office machines .. 100

37. Cell phone etiquette 103

38. Be careful with emails................. 106

39. The impact of the Internet 109

Section VI: Working with Clients

40. The importance of the attorney–client

   privilege. 112

41. Do not judge 114

42. Don't give anyone a blank check on credibility .116

43. Keep a box of tissue on your desk 119

44. Not every attorney is for every client 121

45. Beware of the client who has fired his

   or her first attorney. 124

46. When gender matters 127

47. Should you represent family and friends? . . . 130

48. Make sure you and your client have

   the same expectations 132

49. Don't give guarantees 135

50. Tell your clients they need to follow

   your advice. 138

51. Be specific 140

52. When a client or someone else is in jail 143

53. How to tell whether someone is having

   an affair and why you should care 146

54. How to get your client to tell you the truth. . . 150

55. You may be the only sane person in your client's life. 153

56. Anyone can become crazy 155

57. How to be involved but not overly involved. . . .158

58. Make sure your client has the support of friends and family 160

59. Is the extended family part of the problem or part of the solution? 162

60. Does your client have a safety plan? 165

Section VII: Building a Case and Preparing for Trial

61. Make sure you are suing and serving the right party. 168

62. Look at the jury instructions to prepare your case 170

63. Don't wait for someone to give you information 172

64. Prepare for depositions 174

65. Give mediation a try 176

66. How you know when you have a good settlement 178

67. Hope for the best but prepare for and expect the worst 181

68. Your pretrial settlement discussion with your client 184

Section VIII: Success in the Courtroom

69. Don't throw a fit in court 188

70. Treat the other attorney's client with respect . . . 190

71. Find a nice judge you can talk to 192

72. Research your judge 194

73. Be extremely careful with ex parte communications 196

74. Do these things before you ask the judge for a signature 198

75. How to get your witness ready for court . . . 200

76. You and your client should dress appropriately for court 202

77. How to present your case to the judge 204

78. Tips for picking a jury. 207

79. Cross-examination—you're no Perry Mason . . . 211

80. Know when to sit down and shut up 214

81. Make your record for appeal 216

82. Appeals are a different animal. 218

83. Getting more time in court 220

84. Have a sincere appreciation for
    court personnel. 222

Section IX: The New Lawyer at Home

85. Don't cross-examine your spouse or
    significant other 226

86. Phone calls on nights, weekends, and holidays . .229

87. Find a creative outlet and a physical outlet . . 232

88. Get your affairs in order 234

Section X: Your Legal Career in the Long Term

89. Keep up with your jurisdiction's latest
    ethics and appellate decisions 238

90. Don't let the door hit you 240

91. Why lawyers get burned out 242

92. You have the power to predict the
    future (eventually). 244

93. Stay humble and stay grateful. 246

94. Do not underestimate the power of addiction . .248

95. It's not the crime—it's the cover-up 251

96. Does it pass the smell test? 253
97. You have the ability to change people's
     perceptions about lawyers 255
98. Donate your legal skills 257
99. The importance of defending the
     independence of the judiciary 260
100. Care about politics 263
101. What will people say at your funeral? 265

Conclusion: Why I love practicing law 267

About the Author 271

INTRODUCTION

I went to law school right out of college. Thankfully, I had led a sheltered existence up to that point. My parents were happily married. My siblings were happily married. My friends were happily single. I was young and incredibly naïve. Although I had told people since the fifth grade that I wanted to be a lawyer, I had never even stepped foot inside a law office until a part-time job during my senior year of college.

Maybe it sounds crazy, but I enjoyed law school—well, most of it anyway. I liked the people, I liked my professors, and I liked the classes. But even at law school, I was sheltered. I had little understanding of the practical implications of entering a profession where conflict is everywhere and the seven deadly sins make a daily appearance. After graduation, it became very clear to me that while the study of law deals with statutes, cases, and appeals, the practice of law deals with an intriguing cocktail of greed, substance abuse, domestic violence, and basic immaturity—and that is just between you and your law partners. Your clients also experience these issues in their cases.

That is where I hope this book will be of help to you. Inherent in the practice of law is a significant amount of on-the-job training. By identifying issues and possible trouble spots, it is my hope that students and new practitioners will be better equipped to both successfully represent their clients and also keep a proper balance between the law and their life.

SECTION I:

STARTING OUT RIGHT AT A LAW FIRM

Two dogs are chasing a car and one says to the other, "What are you going to do if you catch it?"

That is exactly the way I felt at the beginning of my legal career. I had been chasing this dream of being a lawyer for so long, and when I had everything I needed—my college degree, my law degree, and my license to practice—I was a little uncertain about what would come next.

Despite the uncertainty you may be feeling, stay positive, pay attention to detail, and work hard. If you can do that, your transition from student to lawyer will be a smooth one.

1.

GET THE DETAILS OF YOUR EMPLOYMENT AGREEMENT IN WRITING

When it comes to their own business affairs, attorneys are notorious for failing to get the terms of their agreements in writing. You would never tell a client to do business on a handshake, so why would you do it yourself? It is important to start your job off right by getting the terms of your employment in writing.

If you are a new attorney, getting the employment agreement you want is a four-part process:

1. Do some research and be prepared to negotiate your agreement. Get to know the Career Services Director at your law school. The director's job is to help both students and graduates find the job they want. He or she will have a wealth of knowledge about the range of salary and benefits you might expect given your education and experience and the size and location of

the firm. If you are going straight into a partnership situation or are office-sharing with someone, you need very specific information from the firm itself about past profits and expenses so that you can determine how future profits and expenses will be shared.

2. Keep an open mind during negotiations. Don't be so set on a particular salary range that you overlook a firm that has amazing benefits or opportunities. That being said, if you work hard, you will be worth every penny the firm pays you, so do not be shy about fighting for the salary you believe you are worth.

3. Get the agreement in writing. If you fail to do this, you make it easier for your employer to avoid living up to his or her part of the deal.

4. Don't sign the agreement until you've had another lawyer look at it. Even if it's a friend or mentor and not someone you've actually hired, it's always a good idea to have a fresh set of eyes check it over.

2.

APPEARANCES MATTER

When I say that appearances matter in your law practice, I am not suggesting that you need expensive suits and expensive cars. My dad says that a bad golfer with nice equipment is still a bad golfer. However, even though it is true that the finest suit will not make you a good lawyer, there is still a certain threshold of acceptable appearance that is expected of you.

Throughout your career, you will see attorneys who should immediately be reported to the Legal Fashion Police. The most extreme example is the attorney who went to visit her client at the detention facility wearing a tube top. That's right, the attorney was wearing a tube top. Even the facility expressed their disapproval of her clothing choice.

So put your tube top away and ask yourself these questions to determine whether or not your appearance is appropriate:

1. *How do I look? When my clients look at me, will they have confidence in me as their attorney? Am I dressed modestly and tastefully? Are my clothes too tight or too loose? Are my teeth clean? Would a judge think I am dressed appropriately?* No one will want to pay thousands of dollars in legal fees to someone who has body odor and bad breath. You are a professional. So look like one. If you have no idea how to do that, go to a clothing store or department store and a sales associate will be glad to help you put some outfits together.

2. *How does my office look? Has my client's file been compiled in an orderly fashion? When my clients see my office, will they have confidence that I won't lose their documents? Do I have stacks of paper everywhere? Are there stale donuts and soda cans strewn everywhere?* To a client in crisis, these are not good signs. If a client comes in unexpectedly and I have a full desk, my assistant and I have a designated spot where we stash the clutter. Avoid shoving it in your desk because you don't want documents to get lost or misplaced.

3. *How does my assistant look? How does her work area look? Is he dressed neatly? Is he or she trying to make*

clients feel welcome and important? The appearance and attitude of your assistant is a direct reflection on you so pay attention.

While expensive clothes and furniture might make a certain first impression, competence and professionalism will make a lasting one.

3.

HAVE EXTRA ESSENTIALS
AT THE OFFICE

Be prepared. You will spend hundreds of hours at your office and you never quite know what the day or night will bring. Will there be pouring rain? Will you have too much garlic for lunch before a big meeting in your small conference room? Will you be sent to court for an emergency hearing? Will a client stop by unexpectedly?

For just such occasions, I suggest you find a small, plain file box to store some essential items that you or someone in your office will most certainly need on short notice. Put it right under your desk so it's there when you need it.

Here's a list of items to start with:

- Various over-the-counter medications, like a pain reliever, cough medicine, cough drops, and cold and sinus medicine.

- Extra toiletries such as a toothbrush, toothpaste, and dental floss. Throw in an extra pair of contact lenses if you wear them. If you are a woman, extra makeup. Consider bringing a blow dryer, curling iron, or hair spray for those last minute touch ups. Good hand lotion is also a must-have.

- A manicure set that includes, among other things, a small scissors, tweezers, and nail file.

- A small sewing kit including a needle, white and black thread, and safety pins. You will learn that you can have wardrobe malfunctions at the most inconvenient moments.

- Generic greeting cards for birthdays and to send your condolences. Sticking a book of forever stamps in the box will ensure these cards actually get sent.

- A compact umbrella.

- Nonperishable snacks for those days when you just can't get away for lunch.

- If you can find the space, an extra suit including shirt, tie, pants or skirt, and shoes. If you are a woman, also include an extra pair of panty hose. You may not have time to run home and change if you are dressed casually and something comes up at the last minute.

With the exception of the extra suit, everything should fit in the small file box. You just may find that you become your office's "go-to" person when life's little emergencies pop up.

4.

WORK WHEN YOU ARE AT WORK

When I tell you to work when you are at work, you might think, "What else would I be doing at work?" It won't take you too long in your office to observe the people who are not actually working. They are making and receiving personal calls. They are checking the scores on the ESPN website. They are trolling for dates on Match.com. They are planning their wedding. They are gossiping with other coworkers. They are taking two-hour lunches.

Let me state a basic truth—Your boss is not impressed by this lackluster behavior. In order to keep your job and advance in your career, impressing your boss is a good thing. Working while you are at work is a good start because you want him or her to think of you as a valuable asset to the office.

Accomplishing this requires you to work diligently to meet and hopefully exceed your boss's expectations. To do this, make sure you fully understand what is expected of you. Here are some questions you should ask and some observations you should make during your first week with the law firm to make sure you understand what is expected of you:

1. *When are you expected in the office in the morning? How long are you expected to stay at night? Are you expected to come into the office on Saturday? Without appearing too curious, take notice of when your coworkers are arriving and leaving to gauge whether your behavior will be seen as acceptable. The managing partner may say, "We don't care when you come in as long as you get your work done," but don't believe it. Find out what the culture in your firm is with regard to the work day and make sure you follow it.*

2. *How many hours are you expected to bill and collect? Are you expected to generate your own clients or will the other attorneys be referring them to you? If you need more work, who do you go to for cases?*

Generally, you want people in your office to see that you are busy. When you're talking to your assistant at her desk for an hour about her vacation, your coworkers see that. When your sister calls you every hour to ask your opinion about her latest boyfriend, your coworkers hear that. Limit the time you spend on the Internet for personal email or shopping. If the office manager has software that allows him or her to see what you are working on at any given time, you don't want to be bidding on an eBay auction.

Another bonus of getting your work done at work is that you can actually be free during your free time. The time away will give you the energy to meet and hopefully exceed expectations both at work and at home.

5.

A TO-DO LIST IS YOUR CONSTANT COMPANION

Being a lawyer is sometimes like being a juggler in the circus. If you can keep all of the balls in the air without dropping one, you're probably doing okay. But if one of the clowns throws in a flaming torch, one of the balls might get dropped.

As a lawyer, you will always have multiple things going on at one time. In one day, your hands may touch a dozen or more files. You are constantly interrupted by the phone and by email. It is a challenge to stay focused and actually complete a task. So here is my simple yet effective solution—always have a to-do list.

Your list should be compiled with input from your assistant at the beginning of each week. The most important function of this list is to spell out for both of you what tasks absolutely have to get done by the close of business on Friday. The list is compiled after the two of you have reviewed your calendar for the next four weeks. What is coming up on your schedule? What hearings do you have? What deadlines are looming?

After you have agreed on the list and decide who is doing what, print out a hard copy and stay in communication with each other throughout the week about what is left on the list. The most pressing items are also placed on the task list on my computer's scheduling program as a constant reminder of what needs to be done. Most Fridays, my assistant and I are scrambling to finish up the last items, but it is comforting to know that we aren't forgetting anything. Regardless of what flaming torches are thrown your way during that week, you can rely on the list to help keep the rest of the balls in the air.

6.

THE IMPORTANCE OF HAVING A GOOD ASSISTANT

Let's begin with two basic truths. First, you are responsible for what your assistant does. It is not your assistant who failed to put a court appearance on your schedule, it is you. It is not your assistant who missed a filing deadline, it is you. The court or your partners do not want to hear an excuse from you about what your assistant did or did not do. It is your responsibility.

Second, your assistant is a direct reflection on you. If your assistant is rude to your coworkers and clients, they will believe you are rude as well. If your assistant is disorganized, you will be considered disorganized as well.

Think of the two of you like a team. We know what the team's ultimate goal is—a good outcome for your client. But what is the game plan? It is much easier to achieve your goal when you and your assistant have similar expectations about what he or she is to do (and not do) and what you are to do (and not do).

Here are your assistant's responsibilities:

1. Always being courteous with clients and coworkers. Rudeness is never appropriate.

2. Making sure your files are up-to-date. If you need to see a document or a letter, you should be able to locate it in the file or on the computer within twenty-four hours from when it came into your office.

3. Staying current on what is going on with your cases. If the case explodes and immediate action is necessary, you will appreciate the time you did not have to spend playing catch-up.

4. Not being afraid to remind you to do things. You should be thankful if your assistant is speaking up because something is not getting done.

Here is how you should act toward your assistant:

1. Always treat your assistant with respect. This should be obvious, but you should never yell or swear at your

assistant. If you are frustrated or upset about something, don't take it out on him or her.

2. Don't ask your assistant to run personal errands for you.

3. Let your assistant know if a coworker or client has commented—either positively or negatively—on his or her behavior. Addressing issues as they arise is much easier than managing issues that have been allowed to fester.

4. Don't forget your assistant's birthday or Assistant's Day.

5. Try not to micromanage. If you have trained your assistant well, then have the confidence to let your assistant do his or her job. Note, though, that despite this, on important matters there is no aspect of the case that is too small for you to oversee and you may need to follow through until the very last step. If you are worried about meeting a filing deadline, your assistant should not be offended if you want to see the receipt from FedEx proving that your documents were sent to the appropriate place by the designated time.

7.

WHEN YOU'RE AN ASSOCIATE, *DRAFT* MEANS *FINAL*

Being an associate at a law firm is a lot like trying out for the basketball team in high school except that the tryout lasts for up to five years. If you play hard and do your best, you hope that you make the team, but it's not a sure thing.

There will be a lot that you don't have control over in your quest for partnership. Here's one thing you do have control over right from day one as an associate—the work you produce. Producing quality work is essential. When a partner asks you for a draft petition, he or she is not looking for something that needs revision. Instead, the partner wants a finished legal document that he or she can submit verbatim.

Here are a few suggestions to make your draft worthy:

1. Make sure you understand the issue. I know that it is sometimes difficult to ask questions because you do not

want to bother the partner. However, if you have missed the boat on what you are supposed to be drafting, the partner is going to be even more unhappy.

2. Keep researching until the very end. Make sure the cases you are citing have not been overturned. Read the advance sheets of the latest appellate cases. If your research is at odds with your position in the case, make sure you discuss this with the partner. He or she is relying on your expertise. Having the opportunity to talk through the case with the partner will be a great learning experience for you and give you some insight into how they evaluate a case.

3. Take an honest look at your writing skills. Your ability to communicate in writing is essential to your success as a lawyer. Pull out your latest writing effort. Are your participles dangling? Are your prepositions hanging? Do you even know what participles and prepositions are? I know you're busy, and you have things you would rather be doing, but I suggest you enroll in a composition class. The benefits will last your entire legal career.

If you produce quality work in a timely fashion, the partners will want to work with you again and again. And when your partnership vote comes up, you'll have strong allies who are fighting to put you on the team.

8.

YOU DON'T KNOW EVERYTHING

My dad has a postcard in his office with a picture of a chimpanzee on it that says, "People who think they know everything are annoying to those of us who do."

I have no doubt that as law school students and new practitioners you are very smart. But being very smart is only one component of being a successful attorney. Successful attorneys also have a healthy respect for the thousands of things they don't know. You need to embrace the fact that there is always something new to learn. Not just about the law, but about yourself, your clients, and your colleagues. Every day is a new day.

When it comes right down to it, thinking that you know everything is really just a type of laziness. When you start working on a new case, don't jump to conclusions and assume you know what the law is. Instead, find the statute and read it. Don't assume you know what the procedural requirements are. Find the rules of civil procedure and read them. You will be shocked at how often attorneys come into court with an inaccurate assumption about the law of the case:

You also don't know everything about your clients and colleagues. Each day at work you see just a small part of what their life is like. Don't assume you know what they are thinking or feeling.

Curiosity and resiliency are important, too. Most lawyers would agree that they have never had two days that have been exactly the same. As a professional, you need to make adjustments to the things you know, the things you don't know, and sometimes even to the things you'd like to forget.

The older I get the more I appreciate how little I know. I truly believe that appreciation has made me a better attorney and a better colleague.

SECTION II:

UNDERSTANDING LAW FIRM POLITICS

One of the most frustrating and unpleasant aspects of practicing law can be the politics of a law firm. Whether you are a lawyer for the government or for a small family firm or for a large international mega-firm, your ability to thrive in this environment will have a huge impact on your career path.

9.

WHEN YOUR LAW OFFICE IS MORE LIKE THE SET OF *SURVIVOR*

Imagine this scenario. A few dozen people are gathered in one place. Unholy alliances are formed. Greed, treachery, and impossible challenges abound. On a regular basis, individuals are voted off and sent home. Is this *Survivor?* No. It's your law office.

What is the best strategy to thrive in this environment? Earn the respect of your coworkers and then fight to keep it.

How can you earn their respect?

1. Work hard. If you are doing your best for the firm, your coworkers will admire you.

2. Accept responsibility when you do something wrong. Don't blame someone else or make excuses. Don't fudge the truth to make yourself look better. Don't involve other people—like your assistant—and ask

them to lie for you. Everyone makes mistakes—even you. So fess up, learn from it, and move on.

3. Stay positive. Congratulate your coworkers on their successes. Acknowledge them when they have assisted in your success. Don't gloat over your own success. If you see that they are doing something wrong, approach them discreetly and help them.

4. Don't gossip. Whether you're in the junior high cafeteria or the law office conference room, gossiping is not a good idea. Here's my classic example of why you should suppress the urge to put your two cents in. I heard through the grapevine that a prominent man in town was having an affair with his secretary. I didn't know the man or the secretary. The topic came up in the conference room at work about the fact that no one knew who this man was having an affair with. For a split second, I thought about saying, "I heard it was his secretary." Thank goodness I kept my mouth shut. The next day I found out that, although the man was having an affair, it was not with his secretary, and, in fact, his secretary was the daughter of someone sitting at the conference table.

If you follow my advice, your behavior will be an example for everyone around. And instead of getting voted off the island, your coworkers may actually want you to stay.

10.

AVOID HAVING A ROMANTIC RELATIONSHIP WITH SOMEONE IN YOUR OFFICE

I'm hoping that this chapter doesn't make me sound like a hypocrite. You see, I had a relationship with someone in my law office and ended up marrying him. Now, eighteen years and four children later, I think that he and I would both agree that having a relationship with someone we worked with was the best thing we ever did.

Generally workplace romances are difficult to pull off without a moderate to excessive amount of drama. My husband and I were fortunate to have a boss who was not going to tolerate drama. After we got married, he called us both into his office, and said: "It's hard to be married and also work together. I don't want your marriage to disrupt this office. If you are fighting at home, you won't be fighting at work." It was our job to be mature enough to keep our personal life out of the office.

Without sounding too much like Dear Abby, if you can't resist dating someone you work with, here are my dating tips:

1. Don't date a secretary or other subordinate employee. This subjects your firm to liability because it could be seen as sexual harassment. You may believe it is completely consensual but when the relationship breaks up, the other person may say that he or she felt pressured. Law firms have enough drama. You don't need to throw sex with your secretary in the mix.

2. Find out what your firm's policy is about coworkers dating and then follow it. If the policy allows a relationship, that doesn't mean you need to advertise the fact you are dating. If the policy forbids a relationship, you can ask for an exception. Whatever you do, don't lie about it to human resources. Don't lie about it to coworkers. If they find out later that you deceived them, they will not be happy.

3. Wait until you've been in your job for a while before dating anyone. Get to know the people at work better before getting to know them in a more intimate

setting. By waiting, you may find that he or she was not what he or she appeared to be at first glance.

4. Don't date a coworker who is married.

5. Don't use office email in the furtherance of your relationship, and avoid excessive personal conversations while in the office.

6. Don't over-share at work. There may be details of your relationship that your other half would not appreciate colleagues knowing about.

7. If you do break up, break up gracefully. A crash and burn breakup could negatively impact both of your jobs.

11.

FOSTER A CLOSE RELATIONSHIP WITH SOMEONE IN YOUR OFFICE WHO HAS YOUR BACK

Working a real full-time job is a new concept for many people coming right out of law school. Although you may have had part-time jobs during school or full-time jobs during the summer, a forty-hour-a-week (or more) job with no Christmas or summer vacation or spring break may come as quite a shock to your system.

What can you do to ease this transition and make your work time less stressful? Find a work friend. Although this sounds simple, it's not. It takes time and it might actually take you a few tries before you find the right one.

Who can be your work friend? Anyone who works in your office. You are encouraged to have more than one work friend. Although work friends of the opposite sex are not strictly prohibited, watch your boundaries. You want to have a work friend, not a work spouse.

What should you look for? Look for someone who will tell you what you need to hear and not what you want to hear. The person who is gossiping in the break room should be crossed off your list. You want the person who will quietly take you aside and say, "I'm not sure if you've heard this, but I think you should be prepared that..." instead of the person who will gossip about you to anyone who will listen. Lawyers love springing things on people, so a little advance notice from a friend goes a long way.

What should you do? To have a friend, you need to be a friend. If you have information that can help someone, give it freely and then keep your mouth shut. If you show someone you are trustworthy, you may find he or she is trustworthy in return. But the key word is "may." Don't assume that because you have good motives that the other person has them, too. Be patient when forming your work friendship so that you aren't shocked if you end up with a knife in your back.

Also, avoid work cliques that exclude others, and try to get to know everyone in your office.

One final comment. A true friend is a treasure. If you are lucky enough to find one, work hard to keep him or her.

12.

IT HELPS TO BE A GOLFER

I know a male lawyer who was notified that his salary was being increased while standing next to his boss in the bathroom. I doubt the female attorneys in the office would receive a raise in salary in the same manner. If you want to advance in your firm, you need to be where the action is. Because you can't go into the men's restroom if you're a woman, you'll have to find other opportunities.

Being a golfer helps. If you don't know how to golf, take some lessons. You might actually enjoy it. You have no idea how many relationships are made and how many deals are done on the golf course and in the club house. You don't have to join a country club to make this happen. Local bar associations usually have at least one golf outing per year and everyone is invited. Many continuing legal education conferences during the summer months will also have an opportunity for people to play golf at the conclusion of the day's schedule.

There are other places to expand relationships, too. The health club, the tennis court, the symphony. Getting to know your fellow attorneys outside the conference room is generally a very good thing.

Did you notice that I said "generally"? I say that because sometimes where the action is is not where you should be. If the action is in a strip club or a bar with drunken colleagues, you will want to politely excuse yourself. You do not want to be considered guilty by association for any of the bad behavior of your fellow attorneys.

On a positive note, I love socializing with attorneys outside the office. Attorneys are funny, well-read, and interesting. Take some time to get to know each other not just for the shop talk opportunities, but because it's just plain enjoyable.

13.

WHAT TO DO IF A COLLEAGUE IS STRUGGLING

A legal career has its share of ups and downs, victories and defeats. Throughout your legal career, you will have colleagues who are sad, upset, or who may even appear to be losing control of their lives or their law practices. Did you know that lawyers experience alcohol abuse and depression at a rate much higher than the general public? When a colleague is struggling, what can you do?

1. If a colleague is struggling with a particular situation, try to get to the bottom of what is going on. I have a friend who calls it the *HALT process. HALT* stands for *Hungry, Angry, Lonely,* or *Tired.* If any of these things are the root of the problem, don't be afraid to talk with your colleague about what is going on. Give him or her the opportunity to share and then help to the extent you are able.

I know a lawyer who fondly remembers his boss reaching out to him after a particularly disappointing jury verdict. The lawyer wasn't as upset about the verdict as he was about the fact that he didn't have anyone to go home and talk with about it. His boss invited him to his home that night to have dinner with his family and the lawyer never forgot that act of kindness.

2. If a colleague's struggles do not appear to be isolated occurrences, look for the warning signs of a more serious problem with substance abuse or depression. Is your colleague drinking during the day? Has he or she ever appeared in court after drinking? Is he or she drinking after work to the extent that he or she is hung-over at work the next day? Are deadlines or appointments being missed? Has anyone else expressed concern about this person?

Keep in mind that your colleague's clients may also be suffering as a result of this. If your colleague refuses to get help, you may need to take further action to ensure that the clients are protected.

3. Give your colleague the phone number of a good counselor. Be prepared for a significant amount of denial.

4. Look for resources at your state bar association. It may be called *Lawyers Helping Lawyers* or the *Lawyers Assistance Program*. Whatever the name, it was created to help attorneys who are in trouble or headed for trouble. Your contact with them is confidential. They are not affiliated with your state's grievance commission. The person who contacts your colleague may even be someone who has gone through a similar experience.

SECTION III:

GENERAL TIPS FOR HAVING A SUCCESSFUL PRACTICE

Your definition of successful practice may be different than mine. To me, a successful practice means a decent living, satisfied clients, quality time with my family, and a good reputation among my colleagues and within my community.

14.

AVOIDING LEGAL PET PEEVES

I asked several attorneys for their pet peeves from the legal profession. While some of them are not huge issues, it will be better for your practice and your career if you understand what types of behavior bother people so you can avoid those actions:

1. *Opposing attorneys who send snotty letters.* Your client receives a copy of all correspondence, and you are the one who must explain—and sometimes make excuses for—an attorney who puts too much attitude and emotion in his or her correspondence. Snotty letters do not advance the case. They only make matters worse.

2. *Attorneys and clients who chew gum in court.* In a quiet courtroom, the echo of smacking gum can drive some folks to the brink of insanity.

3. *Attorneys who misstate the record or misstate the law.* Whether it is intentional or unintentional, you are forced to correct the misstatements. As a result, valuable court time and client retainers are wasted.

4. *Attorneys who fax a letter and expect immediate action.* A fax that arrives on Friday afternoon at 5:00 p.m. and demands immediate action is often impossible to accommodate but still requires attention when you may have other plans.

5. *Attorneys who wear too much cologne or perfume, especially because it makes some people sneeze or gives them a headache.* They seem blissfully unaware of the torture they are inflicting on those around them.

6. *In court, attorneys who address the other attorney and their client by their first names.* Informality can sometimes be perceived as disrespect.

7. *Attorneys who don't return phone calls.* Everyone's time is valuable. An attorney who refuses to communicate with you is being inconsiderate.

8. *Attorneys who treat male attorneys different than female attorneys.* This happens more than people would like to believe.

9. *Attorneys who file sloppy pleadings and briefs.* If you read a pleading and still don't know what the other side wants, it makes writing your response a challenge.

10. *Attorneys who wait to talk to their clients until the last minute.* Talking to your client will allow the case to get settled as quickly as possible. Waiting until the last minute only draws out the process and costs your client more money.

15.

DON'T TOLERATE BAD BEHAVIOR

Each person has a different level of tolerance for the bad behavior of the people around them. For example, some people are not offended by profanity. Some are. Some people are not offended by angry outbursts. Some are. Some people are not offended by insensitive jokes. Some are. As an educated person charged with upholding the ideal of equal justice under the law, I encourage you to have a zero tolerance policy. Even if you are not particularly offended by something, you should protect those in your orbit who may be.

Let's start with profanity. Don't use it. Not to the people in your office, your clients, opposing counsel, anyone. If swearing is a habit for you, it might slip out at a particularly inappropriate time, such as in front of a jury. If you don't swear, people will generally refrain from swearing around you.

Let's move on to insensitive jokes. Don't tell them. Don't email them. If you have any question about what might be appropriate, ask yourself, "If I was part of the group that the joke makes fun of, would I be offended?" If you have any doubt, don't tell it and don't send it. Don't be afraid to tell someone if you have been offended by something. If you do it in a constructive manner, it will be an experience he or she can learn from.

Every once in a while, someone will shock you. The person's behavior will be so outrageous that you are left speechless. This happened to me when a person sitting in my office used an extremely offensive word when referring to another party. It took a second for it to register in my brain that the person had used that word. When it did, I stopped the conversation and said, "You will never use that word in my presence again." He was absolutely stunned but never used that word again.

Never forget that you are a leader and that people will model their behavior after yours. If you expect the highest level of behavior from yourself and from the people around you, you just might get it.

16.

LEARN TO BE A BETTER LISTENER AND A BETTER COMMUNICATOR

There's a story told about J. Edgar Hoover, the former director of the FBI. It is said that the agency was planning to change its stationery. Hoover was shown a proposed sample and he wrote on it, "Watch the borders." For several months thereafter, it was hard to get into the country.

Even when you believe you have been perfectly clear with your client, it's easy for them to get confused. Sometimes our best efforts to communicate with our clients and even the courts go awry. It's important for you to listen carefully and respond clearly.

When you're listening to someone, really listen. If you are talking with someone on the phone, don't answer your email at the same time. If the person is with you in the office, look him or her in the eye and watch for body language. Take detailed notes. If you don't understand something, speak up and get clarification. Keep in mind your client's background and education. Make sure your client understands what you are saying.

As a lawyer, written communication is a daily part of life. If my client was in some emotional distress, I might follow up our in-person meeting with a letter just to make sure the message got through. Something similar happens to me almost every time I leave the doctor's office. I have a hard time recalling what he told me and a follow-up letter would be appreciated. If I am expecting my client to accomplish several tasks before we meet again, I will make a to-do list for him or her and place a copy of this list in the file. That way, my assistant can also see what we are working on if the client calls for help or clarification.

In your written communication, you need to consider your audience. For example, when you are writing an appeal brief, you should always assume that your audience is hostile and that you are going to have to defend each point. When I write a letter to opposing counsel, I always assume that, at some point, the judge may see the letter. Your written communication skills are important so make an honest assessment of your abilities. If you need some improvement, seek out someone in your firm or attend a continuing legal education seminar that focuses on legal writing.

17.

DON'T GIVE ADVICE TO STRANGERS OVER THE PHONE

I'm a bargain shopper. I love to get a good deal on everything from clothes to cars and if I can get something for free, all the better. People needing legal advice will try to get a good deal, too.

Here is a common scenario. A crying lady calls your office and your assistant begs you to talk with her. You don't realize this at the time, but the lady does not have the money or the intention to hire you. She keeps you on the telephone for a half hour telling you her whole story. She then asks you what you think and gets whatever free advice you give her. Six months later you are served with papers. You are being sued for failing to tell her what the filing deadline was and now the statute of limitations has run.

How can this situation be avoided? Be tough. First, your assistant needs to fully understand why you cannot give advice over the phone. You cannot give advice to a stranger over the telephone because there is no possible way that you can gather the facts necessary to give informed advice about the situation. When people like this call, your assistant's standard response should be, "[Insert your name here] does not give advice over the phone. If you would like to set up a time to come into our office, we would be happy to do that."

Second, if the person is very persistent and your assistant tells you that he or she will quit if you don't take the call, your standard response should be, "I do not give advice over the phone. If you would like to set up an appointment, I would be happy to transfer you to my assistant." Although it sounds simple, people in crisis have a way of worming tidbits of legal knowledge from you, so be careful.

Third, document the call. If you end up giving more than the standard response, jot down the date, the name of the caller, and the content of the call. Throw it in a "Potential Client" file. This file serves three purposes. One, if you get sued, you have a paper trail. Two, if the person calls you back in the future and wants to set up an appointment, he or she will be impressed that you remembered what the previous call was about. Finally, if someone from your firm wants to represent the party on the other side of the case, you may need to disclose the telephone conversation to determine if a conflict of interest exists.

18.

RESIST THE PRESSURE TO TAKE A CASE YOU'RE NOT QUALIFIED TO TAKE

Ask yourself this question: Would you let your podiatrist perform brain surgery on you? Unless you were stranded on a deserted island with your podiatrist and were bleeding from a skull fracture, I will assume your answer is no. Knowing that it's important to have a skilled professional with an appropriate level of expertise in the subject matter, why, then, would you agree to take a case that you are not qualified to take? There are three possibilities:

1. Although you currently do not have the expertise, you want to gain experience in that area and are willing to partner with another, more experienced attorney who will guide you through the process. This is probably okay if you are honest with the client about your lack of experience. However, this scenario is still dangerous unless the more experienced attorney knows every

bit of information that you know. Communication will be vital.

2. The client is pressuring you to take the case. Maybe you have done other work for him or her in a different area of the law. Maybe they are your parents' friends. Clients don't seem to realize that a law degree and a law license do not necessarily make you competent to practice in every area of the law. This is where the example of the podiatrist doing brain surgery comes in handy. If you are in a firm where you can refer this client to someone in-house, do that. If you need to make a referral to an attorney outside your office, that's okay, too, and hopefully that attorney will return the favor.

3. The case—and the fee you will receive—look too good to pass up. If this is your reason for taking the case, don't do it. The phrase "money isn't everything" certainly rings true in a situation where you are representing someone in a case and you are uncertain as to how to proceed. You will quickly learn that when you are in a case over your head, you would gladly pay someone else to take it off your hands.

19.

FIND EXPERIENCED LAWYERS YOU CAN TALK TO

I feel fortunate that throughout my career I have had the support and counsel of experienced attorneys. Whether in my firm or my family, I have never lacked for someone to talk to about my practice.

Experienced attorneys can help you with every aspect of your career. From the management of your office to the management of your case to the management of your client, experience is a great teacher. Some attorneys just starting out can turn to others in their firm, but many feel uneasy about asking the other attorneys a question because they don't want it to be used against them. They are made to feel as if asking questions is a sign of weakness or vulnerability.

There are a lot of attorneys who would be great mentors, but they simply aren't looking for someone to mentor. You need to take the initiative to bring these people into your life throughout your legal career. If you are on the same side of the case as an experienced attorney, take the opportunity to study what they are doing and ask questions. Keep track of upcoming trials. Stop in and observe an experienced attorney pick a jury or examine a witness. Follow it up with a telephone call after the trial and ask any questions you might have. Most attorneys will be flattered—and probably impressed—that you thought highly enough of them to watch their performance.

Another way to connect is through your local bar association. Go to the meetings. Take the time to have a cup of coffee if a more experienced attorney wants to chat. Many state bar associations are now taking the lead on mentoring. Because they recognize that new attorneys need support and guidance, they may have a program to match you with a mentor.

We all want to churn out billable hours and impress people with our productivity, but slow down long enough to build relationships. In the long run, developing these relationships is as much an investment in your future as the number of hours you bill.

20.

DON'T PROCRASTINATE

Procrastination is discouraged for law students, but it can be downright dangerous for lawyers. You will learn very quickly that, as a lawyer, you never know what the day will bring. You may think you do, but then someone needs you to cover a hearing, or a case implodes and your schedule is turned upside down. If you add a sick child or assistant to that equation, it's a wonder we use schedules at all.

Despite what I'm telling you, you will disregard my advice and have to learn the hard way that you shouldn't wait until the last minute to do anything. If you wait until the last minute to finish that appeal brief, the copiers will be down. If you wait to prepare your final trial documents until the day before you pick the jury, your assistant will have the flu. Life has a way of interfering with impending deadlines.

To avoid (okay, minimize) these last-minute flurries, I insist on having assistants who are not afraid to pester me. If they know that something is coming up that I haven't started, I want them to put that file under my nose and say, "When are you going to do this?" For your own sanity, you and your office staff need to work together to make sure the work is done on time at a less-than-frantic pace.

Procrastination is also subverted by a well-kept calendar. When discovery arrives at the office or you receive dates for hearings or trials, the deadlines should be immediately entered into your calendar. At that point, you also start counting back to enter additional reminders. For example, if you have a thirty-day discovery deadline in the Smith case, the deadline won't pop up without warning on the thirtieth day. It will also show up on day fourteen with a note that says, "Check on Smith discovery."

An extra benefit of kicking the procrastination habit is that you don't worry as much about the work that is sitting on your desk. Even if you aren't finished with a project, making steady progress gives you piece of mind and allows you to relax when you are away from work. It's when you haven't even started something that the un-done wakes you up at night.

21.

WHAT TO DO WHEN OPPOSING COUNSEL IS A JERK

It has been my experience that most lawyers are reasonably nice people. But as in any profession, there are a couple of rotten eggs. These practitioners seem to revel in making your life miserable. They will send you disparaging letters. They will say bad things about you in front of their client. They will raise their voice and act as if you purchased your law license from the back of the National Enquirer. All of this can be quite upsetting to new practitioners who thought they would be practicing with Atticus Finch and not Ann Coulter.

When dealing with these people, the first thing to remember is that you should not take it personally. Do you really think you are the first attorney they have treated this way? No. They do this all the time so try not to feel too bad about it. You will learn that you need to ignore their behavior and get through the case. Do not give in to the temptation to send nasty letters or emails back to them. Do not lose control of your emotions and get distracted. You should always encourage your clients to take the high road and, in this situation, you need to follow your own advice. Take comfort in knowing that judges are generally quite familiar with the antics of these attorneys and are as unimpressed as you are.

Is there ever a time when you should be more assertive with these attorneys? Absolutely. That time is when they are directing that same bad behavior toward your client in either a settlement conference or in court. Your clients need to know that you will do everything in your power to protect them. If you are in a settlement conference, tell the offending attorney that you and your client will leave if he or she continues to treat you or your client disrespectfully. And then do it. If you are in court, object and hope that the judge intervenes. If not, make a good record so that the appellate court has an accurate picture of the proceedings.

Here is one final suggestion. There is a possibility that this attorney is experiencing some hardship in his or her life that is causing them to act this way. Perhaps he or she is going through a divorce. Perhaps his or her parent or child is very ill. You may get your head snapped off by the reply, but don't be afraid to reach out and ask if everything is okay.

22.

YOU CAN ALWAYS BE
A JERK LATER

I feel very fortunate to practice in a city where the lawyers actually like each other. Our community is small enough that our children go to school together. We know each other's spouses. We see each other at church, at the movie theater, and the grocery store. Being nice to each other isn't something we think about. It just happens. But we don't practice in a bubble. We deal with attorneys from across our state. Some we know and some we don't know. It's important to start off on the right foot with opposing counsel. Here are some suggestions:

1. Make a good first impression. If you are sending a letter, keep it cordial and factual. Don't begin your relationship with this attorney by railing against them or his or her client. Tell him or her that you look forward to talking with them about the case and coming to an acceptable

resolution. When you speak with opposing counsel on the telephone for the first time, be pleasant.

2. When you meet the attorney in person, shake his or her hand, introduce yourself, and smile. Tell the opposing counsel it is nice to meet him or her. If an attorney has a tendency to be nasty, maybe you can signal by that simple step that you aren't impressed with that behavior.

3. Be assertive. Don't beat around the bush about what you want. Being passive or aggressive or passive-aggressive is not in the best interest of you or your client.

4. Don't forget the words of a wise attorney I had the pleasure of practicing with. After receiving a rather abrupt letter from an attorney I didn't know, I went to him for advice about how to handle the situation. Here's what he said: "Start off being nice. You can always be a jerk later." But even on those occasions when an attorney has been rude to you despite your best efforts and you need to take a tougher stand with him or her in order to protect your client's case and your ego, keep it civil.

23.

THINK TWICE BEFORE ACCUSING SOMEONE OF AN ETHICAL VIOLATION

Many attorneys right out of law school have had the experience that a more experienced attorney accuses them of unethical behavior in order to intimidate them. These are usually empty threats. No ethical violation has actually occurred. When this happened to me, I learned shortly thereafter that the attorney was suffering from Alzheimer's disease and that he accused many attorneys of ethical violations. Even though all he did was throw out the accusation, it was still upsetting. Thankfully, real ethical violations that require you to make a report to the state ethics commission are not that common.

Most attorneys are reticent to pursue an ethical complaint against a colleague. Instead of shooting off a letter to the commission in the heat of the moment, an attorney will wait until their emotions have cooled. In the vast majority of these cases, the attorney concludes that the colleague is engaged in what I call "sharp practice" It may not rise to the level that a report needs to be filed, but it's still unpleasant and unprofessional.

If an attorney is accusing you unjustly of unethical conduct, proceed with caution because that is a sign that he or she may be "ethically-challenged." When she gets backed into a corner or he feels the need to deflect criticism away from himself, they question your ethics instead. Communicate in writing with him or her to the extent you can.

Unfortunately, there may come a time when you do need to file a complaint with the grievance commission. Before doing so, talk it over with another attorney if possible. When you make the report, leave out your personal feelings. Just report the facts as you know them. It is not your decision about whether someone will ultimately be found to be in violation. But even in reporting misconduct, you need to be civil and professional.

SECTION IV:

THE BUSINESS OF PRACTICING LAW

For many lawyers, the business of practicing law is a greater challenge than the practice itself. Being a good lawyer does not automatically translate into being a good boss or a successful businessperson. If you are going to make money as a lawyer, you are going to have to put time and effort into the business aspect of your practice.

24.

BE AS INVOLVED AS POSSIBLE IN YOUR LAW FIRM'S FINANCES

On its face, the whole process seems pretty straightforward. Your client pays a retainer. You do the work. You bill the time. The bill is sent. You get paid. Simple, right? Well, not really. There is a great deal of behind-the-scenes activity that ensures your good standing with everyone from the landlord to the IRS to the state bar commission. The role you take in your firm's finances, however, will vary depending on whether you are a partner or an associate and whether you work in a small or large firm.

If you are an associate in a large firm, you may never even see the bills that are sent to your clients. You or your assistant will input your billable time into the computer, and, at a certain time each month, draft bills will be sent to the partner who is overseeing the case. The partner will review the bill, occasionally ask questions of you, and then send out the bill.

Your main job is to make sure you are keeping daily track of your time and that it is entered by the date set by your firm. If you wait several days—or even until the end of your case, as some lawyers do—you will undoubtedly forget about some of the work you did. That is not good for you or your firm. If you consistently fail to have your time inputted into the system by your firm's deadline, the partners will take note.

Although a large firm may have a team of accountants working on everything from collections to monthly expenses, a small firm may only have one accountant or bookkeeper who handles the whole operation. If you are a partner in a small law firm, you need to find simple, common-sense software that both the lawyers and the bookkeeper can understand. Even though you may have no background in finance, you must supervise the bookkeeper. The security of your clients' retainers is an important—even sacred—part of your duty to them. If you review the ethics opinions in your state, you will find many opinions about attorneys who failed to adequately supervise a bookkeeper and client money was stolen.

Whether you are in a large firm or small firm, keep track of your expenses. The written fee agreements for most attorneys contain a provision that you can bill for copies, mileage, telephone calls, and other expenses. If you don't have a system in place for you or your assistant to communicate these expenses to your bookkeeper or accountant, you will lose thousands of dollars each year. Also, give your bookkeeper advance notice if you need checks for payments of court fees and other costs. Don't disrupt your accountant's schedule with your failure to plan ahead.

There are also things that good accountants and book-keepers do to help you:

1. They pay your bills on time and take meticulous care of your trust account.

2. They notify other partners if one of the attorneys is encouraging or insisting upon an irregular practice with regard to a client's money.

3. They encourage transparency in the work that they do.

4. They take a vacation. If your accountant is willing to turn the books over to another person, chances are he or she is probably not trying to cover up any bad behavior.

25.

THE IMPORTANCE OF A GOOD FILING SYSTEM

Paper, paper, and more paper. The rest of the world may be going green, but the legal profession is all about paper. Sure, there are many courts around the country that are transitioning to electronic filings, but the reality for a lawyer is that trees will continue to die for your practice for the foreseeable future.

And what will you do with all of that paper? You will organize it. I would respectfully disagree with the lawyers who believe their files are organized if all of the papers for that particular case get thrown in the same box. If the truth be told, I find a perverse joy in appearing with those lawyers in court. As they rummage through their box trying to find the pleading the judge is referring to, I simply open up my file, flip to the "Pleadings" section, and wait for my colleague to catch up.

To accomplish this in your own practice, you first need to invest in decent file folders. I prefer folders with several sections. The paperwork is punched down at the top of the page using a two-hole punch. In the front cover, I have two documents. My written fee agreement is on the bottom, and a client card containing the contact information of all of the parties is on top. This saves precious time when I need to contact my client, opposing counsel, or anyone else involved in the case. The next section is reserved for written correspondence with your client, opposing counsel, with the court, or with anyone else involved with the case. The letters are organized by date with the oldest letter on the bottom and the most recent on the top. The next section is reserved for important emails from the case. The final section is for pleadings, court filings, and orders. Again, everything is organized by date with the oldest document on the bottom and the most recent on the top. If I have legal research or financial documents such as tax returns or items that may be used as exhibits, I put them in separate, labeled file folders that can simply be tucked into the main folder.

The only thing left to do is the filing. I cannot stress enough the value of opening a file and being reasonably certain that it contains all of the information in a case. Your goal should be to have everything in the file within twenty-four hours of its arrival in your office. Is this always possible? No. But you will understand why this is a good goal when you and your assistant waste valuable time searching all over your office for a document that later turns up under a pile of stuff on your desk. For those times when the file folder is not available, my assistant places the documents in an alpha-betized folder under my clients' last names. This gives the document a safe place to land until it can be placed safely in the file folder.

26.

EARNING A LIVING AS A LAWYER IS A TOUGH BUCK

I remember when I got my first job as an intern in law school. I felt like I was playing dress-up when I left my apartment in my new suit and fabulous shoes. The lawyers I had seen on television were wildly successful and I saw no reason why I would not achieve a similar fate. It did not take long, however, to see that the practice of law would consist of more than dramatic jury trials with witnesses confessing under my brilliant cross-examination.

The title of this chapter is a direct quote from a mentor and law partner. He was a man who spent decades in the practice of law. He had a heart of gold, but he also had no illusions about the life of a lawyer. We try to give our clients realistic expectations about the outcomes of their cases. Ask yourself, "Do you have realistic expectations about the outcome of your law practice?"

Why is earning a living as a lawyer a tough buck?

1. There is a lot of pressure. It's the kind of pressure that bubbles up in unexpected places. It's a pressure that wakes you up at 3:00 a.m. wondering if your assistant filed your responsive pleading on time. It's the kind of pressure that causes some lawyers to slip into alcohol or drug abuse. There is a lot at stake in what you do. Winning and losing often has life-long consequences for your clients and you feel the weight of that.

2. There is a lot of paperwork and hours spent behind a desk. The key to being a good lawyer is to be prepared. Preparation takes time—time away from the other things you would rather be doing.

3. It is not glamorous—it is real life. I have yet to represent a lottery winner. People come to see a lawyer when they are in crisis. A tragedy has occurred. They have been wrongfully terminated. Someone has died. A marriage has failed. They have been arrested. Sometimes the absolute best you—or any other lawyer—can do is to mitigate the impact of

what has happened. You cannot repair what has gone on. Walking your client through their crisis can be described as difficult and rewarding, but it's definitely not glamorous.

27.

HOW TO BUILD YOUR PRACTICE

Whether you are a sole practitioner, an associate with a large law firm, or something in between, generating your own business is a good thing. If you are in practice for yourself, bringing in clients is a necessity. If you are an associate, your ability to bring clients into the firm makes you an even greater asset.

There a couple of obvious hints about how to build your practice, like spending the money for a good ad in the Yellow Pages or creating a firm website which, at minimum, has a brief biography and directions to the office. But when I talk about building your practice, I am talking about more than just advertising your services. I am talking about building relationships.

The first relationship to build is with the legal community in your immediate area. Look for opportunities to meet other attorneys. Find out what kind of law they practice. Be generous in your referrals when you cannot take a case, and they will return the favor.

The second relationship is with your community. Look for opportunities to use your legal skills to help a local charitable organization. Donate your time to do the title work for the new baseball fields, or make yourself available to the local women's shelter when they need a little help. The contacts you make can have long-reaching impact on your practice.

The third relationship is with your region. Many people will travel a great distance to be represented by an attorney they like, so find ways to get your name outside your immediate area. A good way to do this is to become an expert on something. Find an area of the law that interests you, and then learn more about it. Write about it. Look for speaking opportunities, whether it is at the local Rotary Club or the state bar association meeting. Consider reaching out to lawmakers at both the local and state levels. If you have reasoned opinions about pending legislation, your legislators may seek you out when they need advice about legislation.

Building relationships doesn't happen overnight, but holing up in your office will make you neither happy nor prosperous. So get out there and start building!

28.

TREAT YOUR CLIENT LIKE A CUSTOMER

Have you ever been in a fast food restaurant and gotten really bad service? Did the high school girl at the cash register roll her eyes when you asked her to hold the mayo? Were your fries cold? Were you grossed out by the disgusting bathroom? Let's face it. You expect better service than that even though you are spending less than $5.

Now put yourself in the position of the clients at your law firm. What can or should they expect when they are spending thousands of dollars at your business? Do you think they feel they are treated like a customer or an inconvenience?

I had some suspicions about what clients like or don't like, but instead of guessing I thought I would ask several people who had used several different law firms. People who were generally positive about the experience made these comments when asked what they liked about the law firm they used:

- "The people were friendly."

- "The outcome of my case was what I expected."

- "My attorney seemed to care about me and my business."

People who were generally dissatisfied with their experience made these comments when asked what they did not like about the law firm they used:

- "The receptionist was short with me."

- "I didn't get billed regularly."

- "I know I'm not their only case, but I felt like I wasn't important."

What are the lessons we can learn from their comments?

1. You and your staff need to treat your clients with respect. Keep in mind that your clients are on an emotional roller coaster and you are there to help them, not make them feel worse. Every person in

your office from the receptionist to the intern to the runner to the most senior partner, should adopt the "there's no such thing as a stupid question" attitude. Drop the eye rolling and condescending tone.

2. Stay in communication with your clients. They need to know you haven't forgotten about them. When they hire you, tell them that you or your assistant will return their telephone calls within twenty-four hours. Send them copies of any correspondence or court orders you receive on their case. Be attentive to them. Bill them regularly.

3. Keep your office and waiting area tidy. Try this—sit in the spot where your clients sit when they are waiting for you. What do they see? Do they see dust balls and three-year-old magazines? Invest in a subscription to your local newspaper or a popular magazine. Consider putting a television in the waiting area. Make sure someone offers your clients water, coffee, or soda. Occasionally, someone will bring a child into the office, so have some crayons, coloring books, and appropriate toys available. Clean your bathroom daily or hourly if necessary.

Here is the bottom line—your clients need you to give them competent legal advice, but you need your clients, too. They are the ones paying the bills, after all. So treat them well and not only will they come back if they need your help, they will refer their friends and families, too.

29.

GET THE MONEY UP FRONT

As an attorney, you are running your own small business, and you need to get paid for what you do. When prospective clients come to you, they are often in emotional and financial distress, and you may feel uncomfortable discussing your fees with them. I have three words of advice for you—get over it. As difficult as it is to tell someone that you need a $5,000 retainer before you will start the case, it is equally as uncomfortable to explain to your partners or your spouse why you failed to get paid. Here's the reality—hiring a lawyer is expensive. In addition to attorney fees, there are court costs, discovery costs, and office expenses. Your education and training have made it possible for you to provide clients with an extremely valuable service. But do not forget that even though your clients desperately need you now, once their case is over, your fees are no longer their top priority. As many attorneys have learned, attorney fees are dischargeable in bankruptcy.

Here's what you need to do:

1. State clearly and without apology what you charge per hour and how much you need for a retainer. Ideally, you want a retainer that is large enough to cover all of your fees for the case. Tell your client that if any funds remain from the retainer at the end of the case, they will be returned to the client.

2. Prepare an attorney fee contract. Explain it to your client, have them sign it, and give them a copy. Be sure to explain to them that they will be charged when they call you or email you.

3. Don't begin work until the retainer has been received and is in your trust account.

4. Be disciplined about writing down your billable time. If you fail to write it down right away, you may forget to charge for the service you performed.

5. Send a statement of services every month to let your client know what you've done and how much of their retainer is gone.

6. Jump through the necessary hoops and accept credit cards.

30.

HOW TO CLOSE A CASE

What a relief—the judge's ruling has been entered, and the appeal deadlines have run. But you're not quite done yet. It's time to close the case.

Here are the steps you need to go through to do this:

1. Review the final order and make sure everything has been done that was supposed to be done. Were all of the real estate deeds executed and filed? Were the orders dividing the retirement plans approved and filed? Have the court costs been paid?

2. Send a letter to the client saying the matter is concluded and that they should contact you if they have any questions.

3. Organize the documents. Make sure any important emails have been printed and put in the file. If you

want to reuse your expensive file folders, transfer the documents to a less expensive folder.

4. Prepare your final bill for services and make sure you haven't missed any charges for fees or expenses.

5. Understand your firm's system for storing files. Assign it the appropriate number and make sure it is put in the appropriate place. You may need to pull the file at some point, so it is important that you understand where to find it.

6. Find out how long your jurisdiction requires that you store the file and also the financial documents related to how the retainer and fees were handled. Your malpractice carrier may also want to weigh in on how long you keep your files. If you are ever sued, your file would be extremely helpful to them.

Whether it was a big case or a little one, it is a great feeling to put it in its final resting place.

31.

NEVER LET YOUR MALPRACTICE INSURANCE LAPSE

Some people might read the title of this chapter and think, "Attorneys really wouldn't let their insurance lapse, would they?" The answer is yes.

They might do this for a variety of reasons. Maybe they don't have the money to pay the premium. Maybe they are so disorganized that they don't realize the premium is due. They could be depressed and ignoring many of their responsibilities.

Your malpractice insurance is vitally important. Every attorney needs it. No matter how good of an attorney you are, you cannot work without a safety net. A claim doesn't have to be meritorious to be expensive. If you do not have insurance to cover a judgment, your personal assets could be taken.

You also need to take special care when changing firms, changing insurance carriers, or even leaving the practice of law. You should purchase what is called "tail coverage" to make sure there is no gap in coverage and that all of your previous activity remains covered. It can be expensive but you don't have the option not to do it.

You will find that many attorneys are afraid of their malpractice carriers. But almost without exception, your malpractice carrier is your friend and not your enemy. Don't avoid telling them about a possible claim just because you fear your rates will go up. If you do this, you could lose your coverage, because there are time limits for you to report a claim after it has been brought to your attention. The carrier will be glad to talk with you whenever you have a question. Some malpractice carriers also provide free continuing legal education seminars to their insureds. These seminars are both helpful and enjoyable.

You will make mistakes during your career, and you need both the peace of mind and protection that comes with malpractice insurance.

32.

KEEP UP WITH YOUR BILLABLE HOURS

The whole financial system of your law firm is premised upon the two words that strike fear into the hearts of new associates and pain into the pocket books of clients—*billable hours.* Here is the basic premise of the billable hour. Your firm establishes your hourly rate, which is then broken down into increments of tenths of an hour. Your client must pay the firm for each tenth of an hour you work on his or her file. Because you cannot bill the client for bathroom breaks, lunch hours, or for chatting with coworkers about their weekend plans, getting in enough billable hours may be tougher than you think. An eight-hour workday does not equal eight hours in billable time.

Here are seven suggestions to help you bill the required hours:

1. Write down all of your billable time as you perform the work. Even if you just wait until the end of the

day, you will forget to write down that ten minute telephone conversation or the email you received. The lost time can really add up over the course of an entire year.

2. Have a system for keeping track of your time. Some attorneys write it down by hand on a time pad on their desk. Some attorneys keep a document open on their computer all day. They type in the time as they perform the work and email the document to their assistant at the end of the day. Other firms license special computer programs to keep track of your bill-able hours from your computer. Your firm will have a deadline each month by which all billable time must be entered into the system. If you miss the deadline, it will not go unnoticed.

3. Know what your firm's policy is about cutting your time. Many firms say that billable hours are the hours actually billed to clients. For example, if the partner on your case thinks you have spent too much time on a project, he or she may cut your time from twenty hours to ten hours. If that happens, you will only get ten hours of credit toward your yearly goal.

4. Know what your firm's policy is about pro bono work. Many firms say that if you are not getting paid for a case, you will only get credit for half of the hours you actually worked. Even so, it is still a good investment of your time, because it may give you an opportunity for valuable courtroom experience.

5. Know what your firm's policy is about in-house projects, such as case law updates or other writing for the firm that is unrelated to client business. Many firms will only credit you for 75 percent of your time on those projects. Even so, it is still a good investment of your time. Doing a good job can result in more partners asking for your help on their cases.

6. Don't turn away work from a partner unless you are meeting or exceeding your billables.

7. If you are not getting enough hours, you need to talk with partners and other associates to get more work. Do not hide out in your office. If the managing partner questions why your hours are down, you need to be able to show him or her that you made the effort to find work.

In every project you undertake, you must be scrupulously honest when it comes to billable hours. There will always be a temptation to inflate or pad your time. But don't do it. It is unethical and, when it comes right down to it, you are stealing from your client.

33.

LEGAL RESEARCH ISN'T FREE ANYMORE

When I went to law school, we had a huge law library with beautiful books—both new and old. We also had one small room filled with several computers that introduced us to the still-developing technology known as computer-assisted legal research. It didn't take us long to figure out that computer research had definite advantages.

First, it eliminated the frustration of someone misplacing or checking out that one special book you needed to finish your project. Second, computer research was wonderfully fast and efficient. With so much work to do and so little time, the ability to find exactly what you wanted when you wanted it was a relief. Third, every case, every annotation, and every law review was there. The days of waiting for information to come from other libraries was over.

But like so many innovations, computer-assisted research has its disadvantages. In the world after law school, Lexis and Westlaw are not free. Let me repeat—they are not free. Your firm pays for the service, and the charges are passed along to the clients. As a result, you need to have a clear understanding of what is included in your firm's plan. Before utilizing the service, ask yourself whether the charge is a prudent use of your client's limited resources. A client with a relatively small legal matter may not want to pay a large research tab. Maybe you could find the same information for free on the Internet or by looking at an actual book.

Once you have determined that using the computer research service would be helpful to your client, do not forget to log off the service when your search is complete or you get interrupted. It is easy to get distracted when someone walks in your office or you get a telephone call. Also, have the customer service or help line telephone number handy. There are people on call twenty-four hours a day if you are unable to figure out how to get the information you need or need suggestions for your search.

I have one final thought on computer research. There is an old saying, "When all you have is a hammer, all you see are nails." The tools we use tend to dictate how we perform our work. Quick and easy does not always result in a quality work product. You may be able to pinpoint with laser accuracy the specific words you are searching for, but are you overlooking the guiding legal principles that are often more persuasive? Are you looking at the specific code section but failing to look at in the context of the entire chapter? Are you actually reading the cases you are printing off? Anyone can use a computer to locate a case or statute. It takes a lawyer to analyze them.

34.

DISASTER PLANNING

What is your definition of *natural disaster?* I would submit that *natural disaster* for most people is defined as, "something that happens to other people." But guess what? Despite your wishful thinking, natural disasters can happen to you and they can happen to your law practice. Maybe you live in a part of the country with earthquakes, wildfires, or hurricanes. For me, it was a flood that forced me out of my office for four months. For my friend, it was a tornado that blew apart his law office in a matter of seconds. We prepare our clients for worst-case scenarios, so make time to prepare yourself and your practice. Here are a few simple questions to get you started:

1. *What sort of client information do you have in your office?* If you have original wills, abstracts for real estate, or other one-of-a-kind documents, buy a fireproof safe and keep it in a closet or other protected area.

2. *Do you have off-site backup of the information on your computers?* If you back up your files but keep the information in your office, it is of no help to you if your office is destroyed. Check with your state bar association. They may offer off-site back up for a small fee.

3. *What sort of insurance do you have and where is your policy kept?* Check out three specific kinds of insurance. The first is called *business interruption insurance* (BII). BII guarantees lost income and profits you would have earned if not for whatever caused the interruption. Buy it with the fewest exclusions possible even if it means paying a little higher premium. The second is called *extra expense coverage.* This will reimburse you for operating at a different location while yours is being repaired. The third is called *valuable papers or records insurance.* This will cover the cost to replace one-of-a-kind documents that may have been destroyed.

4. *How would you communicate with your partners, colleagues, and staff in an emergency?* Keep an accurate list of addresses and cell phone numbers both on-site and off-site. In situations where Internet service is interrupted, your cell phone will be your lifeline.

5. *If you had one hour to remove items from your office, what would you take?* Create a list of what the priority items would be. For example, you may decide to grab the computer hard drives but leave the monitors behind. Make sure key people are aware of the list so the evacuation plan can be put into place regardless of who happens to be in the office.

If a natural disaster strikes, in all likelihood, you won't be the only one affected. Your clients, friends, family, church, and schools may also be impacted. Your entire community may be suffering both emotionally and financially. The time you have spent in advance to prepare your law office will give you greater freedom to provide comfort and assistance to those who need it.

SECTION V:

BECOMING COMFORTABLE WITH TECHNOLOGY

Technology is great, but in the practice of law, no matter how hard we try, technological gadgets will never be a substitute for careful preparation and research. Technology will not make you a good attorney. However, when used appropriately, it will make a good attorney even more efficient.

35.

STAY ON TOP OF TECHNOLOGY BUT DON'T BE A SLAVE TO IT

Do you know what a luddite is? A luddite is a person who resists technology. At the turn of the nineteenth century, the luddites in Great Britain were smashing textile machines to halt the march of progress. There are people in the legal community who consider themselves luddites. Believe it or not, there are still lawyers and judges out there who have no idea what a Google search is.

On the other extreme are lawyers who are technology addicts. Whatever the gadget, whatever the cost, they need the best and the fastest. They spend hours researching and reading about what is the latest and greatest. The problem with that is that there will always be something better, so it's a never-ending cycle of expense and dissatisfaction.

My belief is that both ends of this spectrum need to work their way toward the middle. Whether it is e-filing documents or Power Points for the jury, technology is here to stay.

Here are three technology must-haves:

1. *The ability to access your email from your cell phone.* Even if you don't want to use it very often, it may be vital if a client has an emergency or a case implodes.

2. *A wireless synch of your schedule between your cell phone and your computer.* Having an up-to-date view of your calendar is valuable when you are out of your office and trying to set dates with the court, your client, or another attorney.

3. *A small but quick laptop computer with Microsoft Office and a zip drive with plenty of space.* The computer gives you the ability to create documents regardless of your location and the zip drive gives you the ability to get them printed.

A word of warning about your gadgets. You have to know when it is appropriate to use them. I know of at least one attorney who has been sanctioned by the court for playing games on his computer when he should have been participating in a hearing. Similarly, sitting at counsel table is not an appropriate time for text messaging.

36.

KNOW HOW TO OPERATE THE OFFICE MACHINES

I know what you're thinking. You have seven years of higher education. You are paid $200 per hour. Time is money. You don't need to know how to work the office machines.

Here is why your thinking is flawed. The law is all about deadlines. You have to do a certain thing by a certain date. That's the way the court system functions. What happens if your assistant is not available—he or she is sick, had an emergency, is on vacation—and you have a deadline to meet? Guess what? Other people in your law office have deadlines to meet, too, and so they may not be able to loan their assistant to you at the minute you need one. Or maybe you are in the office at night preparing for a trial or hearing which is starting promptly at 9:00 a.m. What if you need twenty copies (collated and stapled) and the copier jams? What if your computer crashes? What if the ink in the fax needs to be changed? Will you know what to do?

Here are the machines that you need to know how to use without anyone's help:

1. *The copier.* You should know how to make copies and change the toner when it runs out. You should also know where to look when you are trying to find the one sheet of paper that is jammed somewhere in the machine.

2. *The dictation equipment.* You should know how to work your end and also your assistant's end. If another person is trying to help you get a letter out when your assistant isn't there, you may have to give a quick tutorial about how to work it.

3. *The fax machine.* Even in a world where email and attached documents are more and more prevalent, the fax machine is still a constant companion. Learn how to fix a jam. Learn how to change the ink. Do you even know where the paper is kept?

4. *The computer printer.* I'm going to assume we all know our computers well enough to work with those. But

what about your printer? Is it in a remote location? If you need a document right now and can't email it to someone else to print, consider having a back up printer that you can hook up directly to your computer if the network printers aren't working. At a minimum, keep a zip drive handy so that you can print your document elsewhere.

5. *The typewriter.* Yes, it's true. People still use typewriters. Whether it's for a form that needs to be filled out or something else, you should find out where the type-writer is, where its on switch is located, and where the white-out is.

37.

CELL PHONE ETIQUETTE

Does anyone even remember what it was like before cell phones? Do your remember trying to find a pay phone? Or calling someone collect from someone else's phone? Or how about the prepaid phone card? Thankfully, those days are over forever. But there is a downside. Your cell phone is an ever-present part of your life. We are constantly confronted with people who, by their sheer proximity to us, force us to endure the blow-by-blow of their disappointment with their manicurist or their rants about their latest boyfriend or girlfriend. But, while these people are obnoxious, there is no client-manicurist privilege so there is no restriction on the world hearing their entire conversation. As a lawyer, you are in a different situation so what should you remember when using your cell phone for work?

First, always be conscious of the attorney-client privilege and what information you are revealing to the people around you. Contrary to popular belief, you are not surrounded by an imaginary telephone booth that prevents others from hearing your conversation. My assistant and I have a running joke that my clients only have emergencies when I am getting my hair washed at the salon. If my assistant needs an answer right away and I am in the middle of the scalp massage, it is not inappropriate to give a short answer that does not give specific information regarding the name of the client or any identifying details. However, if the answer requires any more than that, I should probably excuse myself to a private corner for the remainder of the conversation.

Second, give your cell phone number to your clients at your own peril. If you tell them the number is for emergencies only, you will quickly find that their definition of emergency and your definition are two entirely different things.

Third, for those of you who have children, be careful about the phone conversations you have in their presence. Even if they are busy watching television, you would be surprised at the information they are absorbing. If you say to your spouse before work, "I have a rough day today," and your ten-year-old interjects, "Is today the day you are trying to get that dad to pay his child support?" you're probably not paying enough attention to what your kids are hearing.

Fourth, turn your cell phone off when you enter the courtroom. Let me say it again: turn your cell phone off when you enter the courtroom. If your cell phone rings during court, it disrupts the entire proceeding and judges do not like it. Let me say it again: judges do not like it. If you forget and leave your phone on and your phone rings during court, don't answer it. Let me say it again: don't answer it. Just turn off the ringer, apologize profusely, and pray that the judge doesn't find you in contempt.

38.

BE CAREFUL WITH EMAILS

When I first started practicing law, no one used email. Those were the good old days of letters and telephone calls. But the world has changed, and email is here to stay. Here are some things to remember when using email in your practice:

1. Get specific permission from your clients to contact them via email. They may not want you to send email to them at work or if other people have access to their account. I have a line on the bottom of my client card that I have my clients sign regarding whether they want to communicate by email.

2. Make sure your clients know that they will be charged for emails. Some clients have the mistaken impression that if they are not sitting in your office or in a court-room, then the clock is not running.

3. In emails to your clients, do not make disparaging remarks about the other attorney or the opposing party. Emails have a way of getting around, so you need to stick to the facts and not get sidetracked.

4. Remind your clients that all of the emails they send to anyone in the case (other than you), may be come back as evidence. So if they emailing their soon-to-be ex-spouse, they should ask themselves whether that is the tone and content they want the judge to see.

5. Print hard copies of important emails and include them in the file.

6. Don't forward chain letters, jokes, or anything similar from your work email. You don't know who is going to be offended by what, so the best practice is just not to do it.

7. Don't assume your email has been received. It could have ended up in their spam folder. So instead of getting huffy about their non-response, resend it or actually pick up the telephone and call.

8. Try not to read too much into emails. When you talk with your clients or other attorneys in person, you can hear how they are saying something, but over email it can be easy to misinterpret how they intended their statement. Instead of shooting back a snotty email yourself, call them on the phone to see if your initial impression was correct.

9. Beware of programs that insert email addresses after only typing a few letters. It may insert the wrong address without you realizing it and you could send a confidential email to the wrong place.

10. Don't delete your emails without knowing what your office policy is regarding their archiving and retention. Some firms archive emails automatically after six months and some do not. Although you need to periodically clean out your emails, you don't want to get rid of something that you were required to keep.

39.

THE IMPACT OF THE INTERNET

One of the biggest changes during my legal career has been the impact of the Internet on our daily lives. It's been my observation that people who grew up without the Internet are a little surprised at the lack of privacy. Through social networking sites like MySpace or Facebook, people share intimate details of their life with friends and strangers alike. For the post-Internet generation, this is simply a fact of life. It's the way they stay in touch with friends. I'm sure they think that life was terribly boring without these sites.

But the reality is that the sheer amount of information on the Internet makes it a fertile ground for finding out information about the parties and witnesses involved in your case. When you start a case, you need to ask your client what they have posted on their Internet sites. If there is anything that a judge or jury may find offensive, it should be taken off immediately. I also tell them not to talk about the case or the other parties on anybody else's site. I tell clients that they should not post pictures of their children on those sites. There are just too many weirdos out there, and a judge may question their judgment.

I also ask my clients about what the opposing party and their witnesses may have posted on their Internet sites. You can get some interesting and useful information. Tell your client that every attorney and every client is looking on the Internet for information about the other side and they should act (and type) accordingly.

Take a minute and Google yourself. What will your clients or potential employers find when they are searching your name? Your professional reputation may not be enhanced by photographs posted of you partying at your cousin's wedding. You should also be careful with blogging. Although talking about the law in general is acceptable, responding to a stranger's question with a specific answer may subject you to a malpractice claim or, if they reside in another state, a claim that you are engaged in the unauthorized practice of law.

SECTION VI:

WORKING WITH CLIENTS

As an attorney right out of law school, developing healthy and constructive attorney-client relationships will be a challenge. A healthy relationship means that you have the confidence to tell your client what he or she needs to hear instead of what they want to hear. A constructive relationship means that you have the ability to guide your client to the best possible outcome.

40.

THE IMPORTANCE OF THE ATTORNEY-CLIENT PRIVILEGE

We all know the attorney-client privilege is important. It's so important that every state has a law protecting it. It's so important that you will be severely punished by your state bar commission if you violate it. Loose lips sink ships and they can do the same thing to your law practice. So in your real life, what does the attorney-client privilege mean?

First, it means that everyone in your office must place the same importance on the privilege as you do. Your legal assistants, your runners, your custodians—it must be clear to everyone that no client confidences will be broken. If your client knows someone who works in your office or has a social relationship with them, he or she must be able to trust that personal information will not be available for public consumption. In that situation, I personally remind the person in my office that he or she is not to say anything or acknowledge anything about the case to anyone. Period.

Second, it means that your office should be set up in a way that doesn't inadvertently convey information to other people. When you have someone in your office, are there other files out with client names on them? When your receptionist answers the phone, can the person in the waiting area identify who is calling?

Third, it means that your spouse or significant other cannot know everything about your cases. The privilege is so important that you cannot risk violating it. I had a client come into my office and say that she had seen my husband at the grocery store and that she was surprised that he didn't know that she and her husband had separated. I told her that the reason for that was that her information was confidential and I didn't tell him. Trust me, most spouses are better off not knowing especially in situations where they know the parties.

Finally, without the attorney-client privilege, your relationship with your clients would be compromised to the extent that you could no longer effectively assist them. So think of the privilege not as a heavy burden but as a precious gift to be protected and preserved.

41.

DO NOT JUDGE

The first universal truth I learned as a young lawyer is that you never know what is going on in someone else's life. This truth impacts the impression you give your clients. When you sit across the desk from an affluent, church-going lady, what will your facial expression be when she tells you that her husband is addicted to Internet porn? How will you react when a mild-mannered gentleman enters your office and tells you that he embezzled thousands of dollars from his employer?

Always remember that you are there to help—not judge. The reasons people keep secrets vary. Sometimes they are motivated by shame or worry of being socially ostracized. Most know that if their secret is publicly outed that their lives will change. Consider the courage it took for them to come to your office and talk with you. After suffering in silence for a long time, they finally made a decision that their secret was just too big for them to handle.

This truth is not limited to your clients. It also extends to your colleagues, friends, and acquaintances, so be sensitive about your comments. For example, tread lightly when condemning people who have extramarital affairs because the person sitting next to you may be involved in one or be the victim of one. Your comment could increase their shame and make it even more unlikely that they will reach out for the help they need. The same holds true for addiction or mental illness or any of a variety of problems that people are reluctant to open up about. You never know the situation of the person you are talking to, so proceed with caution when expressing your opinions.

Whether it is your clients or your colleagues, never forget that it is an honor to have someone confide in you and then trust you to help. If that is truly your attitude, you will never lack for either.

42.

DON'T GIVE ANYONE A BLANK CHECK ON CREDIBILITY

One of the unfortunate consequences of being an attorney is that I have a hard time believing anyone is being 100 percent truthful. Even a person who is telling the truth is still looking at the situation through his or her own lens and will not see the situation in the same way that a neutral observer would. So how do you know when someone is lying? How do you know when a fact has been inadvertently omitted versus intentionally left out?

You will find in your law practice that there are certain phrases that immediately raise a red flag regarding credibility. These phrases include the following:

• "I only had two drinks."

• "I was just minding my own business when..."

• "I don't have any idea how that got there."

Absent one of these phrases, you may have to dig deeper to determine who is telling the truth. A judge will tell a jury that they can't draw any conclusions from the evidence until they have heard both sides of the case. The same is true for you in your practice. You need to stay open to the facts of the case until you have enough information to start drawing conclusions. Don't assume that because your client is of a certain social standing that he or she is telling the truth. Don't assume that because your client is crying that he or she is telling the truth. Don't assume that because it is your client he or she is telling the truth.

Here are a couple of suggestions to get some insight from your client about what the other side is going to say:

1. As you begin your initial consultation, tell you clients that you need them to tell you the truth. My favorite phrase with clients is, "It is what it is." I tell them not to worry about the legal impact of the facts—that's my job. I also tell them that usually the consequences of them telling the truth are not as bad as they think it will be. For example, some people in a divorce case are terrified to tell you that they have had an affair. What they don't realize is that you are not there to

judge them, you are there to help them. And you can't help them if the first time you hear about their affair is during their cross-examination in their child custody trial.

2. Ask your client, "What is the other party going to tell their attorney about you?" This question often gets out some of the more uncomfortable information they may not have felt they could tell you at first.

3. Remind yourself to keep a healthy amount of skepticism regarding everyone involved in your case. If you get lazy about finding the truth, you may find yourself in an uncomfortable position when the actual facts are different from what you had assumed they were. It's just good practice to say, "Maybe I don't have the whole story," and then get to work finding out what that story is.

43.

KEEP A BOX OF TISSUE ON YOUR DESK

After my first year of law school, I interned with a terrific firm. They had a lot of lawyers practicing a lot of different kinds of law. After I indicated to one of the attorneys that I was interested in divorce law, I was promptly summoned to the office of the cigar-smoking, crusty senior partner. I had barely sat down when he leaned over the desk through a cloud of smoke and said, "Why in the world would you want to do divorce law?" I'm sure I mumbled something about wanting to help families through a crisis. He interrupted me and said, "When you do divorce work, there are two things you should never forget. Everyone is poorer after a divorce, and always have Kleenex on your desk."

I'll admit the significance and complete truth of his statements were completely lost on me at the time. But now I realize he knew exactly what he was talking about.

It is hard for people to watch their hard-earned assets be callously split in two by expensive divorce attorneys. As much as your client insists that he or she is getting the short end of the stick, the reality is that both parties are getting the short end of the stick. Everyone will leave the marriage financially worse off than when they were married. And that's hard to take sometimes. I tell my clients that if they and their spouse are equally unhappy with the outcome, then it's a probably a pretty good settlement.

When the senior partner advised that I should keep Kleenex on my desk, my immediate thought was, "Why would someone pay a lawyer an enormous hourly rate and then spend their time in his office crying?" I have come to realize that it is because the facts you both must deal with are requiring them to face the reality of their situation—if only for that hour or two. You are playing a huge role in one of the saddest and most significant events of their life. So let them cry, and don't forget to keep an extra box of Kleenex under your desk just in case.

44.

NOT EVERY ATTORNEY IS FOR EVERY CLIENT

Have you ever gone to a doctor who you really didn't like very much? Maybe it was his or her bedside manner. Maybe you had to wait too long. Maybe there were really old magazines in the waiting room. On the flip side, have you ever gone to a doctor who you felt didn't like you very much? Maybe you asked too many questions. Maybe you complained that you waited too long or that the magazines were too old. Whatever the reason, a strong connection wasn't made. This failure to connect may not matter if you were going in to have your cholesterol checked, but what if you were really ill? Would you still want that same doctor? Would they still want you as a patient?

Just as it is true that not every doctor is for every patient, not every attorney is for every client. Some attorneys are under the mistaken impression that if a client comes into their office and has the ability to pay, they are under an obligation to take the case. They aren't. The decision about who your clients are is a two-way street. I tell prospective clients at an initial consultation that we both get to make a decision—they get to decide if they want to hire me and I get to decide if I want to take the case.

This story does not end, however, when the fee agreement is signed. What happens when there is a breakdown in your attorney-client relationship when the case is pending? It doesn't happen very often, but there will be times throughout your career when you and/or your client seriously question whether you should be the attorney in the case.

In that situation, be honest with yourself about the source of the problem. If it's just that your client is mildly annoying, you can tough it out. But is it something more serious? On your client's side, has something happened that has caused them to lose confidence in your ability to represent them? As difficult as it is to talk about, I suggest discussing this openly with your client. Your conversation may start out with something as simple as, "Are you satisfied with the way your case has been handled so far?"

At some point during your career, it is almost inevitable that you will get taken off a case by a partner or fired by a client. Although you could simply chalk up the unfortunate ending to a personality conflict, I suggest you dig a little deeper in order to learn from the experience. What could you have done better? Were there warning signs you should have paid more attention to? Ultimately, the most important lesson may be to trust your instincts at that initial client meeting, and either flat out refuse to take the case with a questionable client, or ask for a retainer so huge that you won't mind suffering a little.

45.

BEWARE OF THE CLIENT WHO HAS FIRED HIS OR HER FIRST ATTORNEY

There are many times throughout your career that you will think, "I wish I hadn't taken this case." You and your spouse or significant other agree that there is no amount of money that would have made this case worth it. You swear you will never again be in that position but you are.

When you get tired of practicing law this way, ask yourself a simple question, "How could I have avoided this?" As you made your decision whether or not to accept the case, were there any warning signs that this case was going to make you dread going to work in the morning? Sometimes you can honestly say no and that the volcanic eruption of your case was a complete surprise. But most of the time your case was spitting ash from the moment it walked in the door and you simply failed to recognize it.

So what is the number one warning sign that, at some point, your case will be draining your existence of its life force? The number one warning sign is a client who has fired his or her previous attorney during the middle of the case. As with most of my advice in this book, there are always exceptions. I'm sure we can all name attorneys that we would congratulate a client for dismissing. But generally, if you know this attorney to be generally competent, the fact that they got fired during the middle of the case should make you run in the other direction.

What may this suggest?

1. That the client has trouble following the attorney's advice. Think of the child that runs to Dad when Mom says no.

2. That the client thinks he or she is smarter than the attorney.

3. That the client cannot pay the attorney.

Make no mistake, none of these things bodes well for your case.

So if someone wants to fire their attorney and hire you, I suggest you do the following:

1. Encourage the person to try to work things out with his or her current attorney. Tell the person to talk openly about his or her concerns with the other attorney.

2. Do not disparage the other attorney. If you would have done things differently that's okay, but speak in a respectful manner about your colleagues. Remember, you don't know that side of the story.

3. If the person still can't work it out after talking with his or her current attorney, tell the potential client that you need an enormous retainer. If he or she pays it, great. You are assured of getting paid. If not, great. You have just saved yourself from being sacrificed to the volcano.

46.

WHEN GENDER MATTERS

I understand that some people may take offense to me even raising this topic. They might ask, "Why would it make a difference what gender your attorney is?" Don't get me wrong, it usually does not make a difference. However, there are certain fact situations with certain clients that your gender—male or female—comes into play.

Consider this scenario. A woman has lived her entire life being emotionally or physically abused by men. It started with her father and continued with her boyfriends and husband. She feels worthless and helpless. Not just a little but a lot. Not just occasionally, but most of the time.

This same woman is now getting divorced. As her attorney—who also happens to be female—you try to give her advice on everything from custody to property division. Only with great reluctance will she follow your advice. She questions the basis for your opinions more than any other client you can remember. She double-checks whatever you say with anyone who will listen and then still doesn't seem quite satisfied.

What is going on here? Let me tell you. This woman has lived her whole life being told that women are weak and worthless. In her life, every move is approved of and controlled by men. Only intensive and extensive therapy will make her see that she associates men with power and women with weakness. Unfortunately and inaccurately, she believes that you, as a woman, are not capable of doing your job. In her eyes, you are weak like her.

You can't cure her of this. You're not a therapist and, even if you were, you don't have enough time. So what do you do? You find a caring, respectful male attorney to handle her case. Make sure this is a colleague who returns phone calls and has a great deal of patience with his clients. Make sure that he is smart and will give her good advice because whatever he says, she will most likely do without hesitation.

There are also clients—both male and female—who will hire an attorney of the opposite sex for the purpose of manipulating them or the situation. The male client, for example, may be trying to soften his image by hiring a female attorney. You as the attorney need to be careful not to let yourself get into sucked into a bad situation by a con artist.

47.

SHOULD YOU REPRESENT FAMILY AND FRIENDS?

I have a sister who is a nurse. On health matters, both big and small, she is my go-to gal. I've relied on her advice on everything from tonsils to concussions to broken limbs to childbirth. She has never asked for a dime for sharing her expertise and I have never expected her to make an official diagnosis or open up an urgent care clinic in her living room.

Similarly, your family and friends will come to you for advice on legal matters both big and small. Ninety-nine percent of the time you will be honored they asked and thrilled to offer whatever guidance you can. Maybe your cousin is getting divorced or your friend's grandmother died without a will. Most family and friends will be satisfied with general advice and maybe even a few phone calls to find a great referral for them. But some will actually want to hire you. So what happens then?

You have two choices. You can just say no. You can explain that you wouldn't represent yourself. That part of what you bring to the process is a dispassionate view. If your feelings are too closely tied to the client, you may not be able to effectively represent them. The witnesses may also be relatives. Do you really want to cross-examine Aunt Muriel?

You also have the option of saying yes. If you want to do it and your firm is okay with it, there is nothing preventing you from doing so but beware that problems may arise at any point.

A better option may be to have another attorney in your firm take the lead on the case.

One final word. Be careful not to share your family member's information with the rest of your family. Even if he or she is not officially hiring you, make it clear that you will not tell the rest of the clan about whatever difficulties that person is experiencing. If that person wants to share, that's fine. But your family member needs to know that the information will not come from you.

48.

MAKE SURE YOU AND YOUR CLIENT HAVE THE SAME EXPECTATIONS

Sometimes it's hard to have tough conversations with your clients. You beat around the bush. You put things in the best possible light. You try to break it to them gently. This is all well and good but you still have to give them the best possible information in a way they will understand it.

Let's divide the expectations into four different categories—your expectation for their behavior, their expectation for your behavior, the expectation of the attorney fees, and the expectation of the outcome.

What is your expectation of their behavior? You tell them that:

1. you expect them to return your phone calls and respond to your letters;

2. you expect them to notify your office if they change their address or phone number;

3. you expect them to call ahead and make an appointment because just popping in your office without one may not work with your schedule; and

4. you expect them to follow your advice.

What is their expectation of your behavior? You tell them that:

1. you or your assistant will do everything in your power to return their phone call within twenty-four hours of receipt of the message;

2. you will answer their questions;

3. you will provide copies of all correspondence and court filings to them; and

4. you will bill them on a regular basis.

What is their expectation of the attorney fees? This is where a written fee agreement comes in very handy. When you go through it, you can talk in detail about what they will be charged for. I try to estimate what fees might be and I try to estimate high. Don't soft peddle around just how expensive it is to hire an attorney.

What is their expectation for the outcome? I make sure they understand the range of possibilities regarding whatever kind of case they have. At the beginning, I give them the minimum and maximum possible outcomes and then, throughout the case, I keep them updated about where things are headed.

49.

DON'T GIVE GUARANTEES

Do you have a "Satisfaction Guaranteed" sign hanging in your office? How about a sign that says, "If not completely satisfied, please return within thirty days for a full refund"? Of course you don't. But even if these signs are not hanging on your door, the message may be in the air.

Early in my career, someone charged with a crime came in my office for an initial consultation. He explained the facts of his case and asked, "Can you get the charges dismissed?"

I said, "It looks like you have a good case but there is so much more I need to know before I can give you an opinion about that. To start, I need to read all of the police reports and interview the witnesses."

He replied, "Well, I have already talked with [insert lawyer's name here], and he guaranteed me that he could get the charges dismissed."

My reply: "Then I think you should hire him!"

And he did. Several months—and I'm sure several thousand dollars—later, I ran into him and his attorney at the courthouse where he had just pled guilty to the charges.

The moral of the story? Never give guarantees about the outcome of a case. I repeat: Never give guarantees about the outcome of the case.

Your clients will push you for a guarantee because they don't understand how unpredictable the legal universe can be. Don't get cornered by clients into promising more than you can deliver. Tell them two things to keep them grounded in reality. First, tell them the minimum and maximum they can expect. For example, if your client has been charged with contempt, the minimum may be a dismissal with the other party paying their attorney fees. The maximum may be a jail sentence, a fine, and payment of the other party's attorney fees. In order to properly evaluate the risks they are facing, you need to be clear with your client about what the range of possibilities are.

Second, tell them that any time someone goes into court asking for something, there is a chance they are going to get it. The judge or jury is the final arbiter of what the outcome is—not the attorneys and not the clients. If they think they have a slam-dunk case, you better help them to think again, because the folks making the decision may have a different idea.

50.

TELL YOUR CLIENTS THEY NEED TO FOLLOW YOUR ADVICE

Different lawyers have different philosophies about how they interact with their clients. Some lawyers view themselves as a mouthpiece for their client. Whatever the client wants, however ridiculous, they believe it is their job to ask for it. What is the downside of this philosophy? It damages your client's credibility and it damages your credibility. Your client looks unreasonable and delusional and you look like you don't understand the law, you have no client control, or both.

So if it's not in the client's best interest or in the attorney's best interest to let the client dictate the legal strategy and argument, why does it still happen? I'll tell you. It happens because attorneys are too timid about telling their clients what they should do. If the client perceives that they are driving the bus, they will roll right over you.

Here's how I avoid this. In the initial consultation, I tell the client, "You have hired me to give you legal advice. When I give it to you, I expect you to take it." I then tell them the story of a client who asked this question in her initial consultation: "Are you a good attorney?" My response? "Yes, I am a good attorney. But if you do what I tell you to do, I am a great attorney." She went on to be one of my favorite clients even though it was a very difficult and emotional case. And, yes, she did what I told her even when she didn't want to, and we ended up with the outcome she wanted.

That being said, there are situations when I don't tell the client what to do. There are times when we have several paths we could take without either of us looking ridiculous in court. At that point, I view it as my job to lay out the options and possible outcomes and then let the client decide how we proceed. It is his or her life after all.

When you are a new attorney, client control is hard, because you don't have the confidence in your legal knowledge or experience to fight for what you believe your client should do. Just hang in there. As the months pass and you work on more and more cases, your confidence will grow, and soon you will feel comfortable knowing when and where to put your foot down.

51.

BE SPECIFIC

When it comes to a contested legal battle, you will find that people get very defensive and will look for ways to avoid telling you something. If you ask someone to tell you the truth, do you think their definition of "truth" is the same as yours? Is their definition of *is* the same as your definition of *is*? There is no way to avoid this hair-splitting. However, if you can pin people down to the extent you are able, their nuanced responses may give them serious credibility problems later.

Let me give you a classic example. You have a child custody case where your client's wife accused him of having an affair. He emphatically denied this and cried and carried on in your office to the extent that you didn't dig any deeper than that. At the trial, on cross-examination, opposing counsel asks him, "Isn't it true that you had sex with Jane Doe when your wife was home watching the kids?" Much to your shock, his response is "Yes." When his cross-examination is complete and he walks back to counsel table, you ask the judge for a moment to speak with your client. With your legal pad held up to shield you from both the judge and the other attorney, you whisper, "You said you had never had an affair!" He calmly responds, "It wasn't an affair. It was a one night stand." Lesson learned.

To avoid such an incident, I do two things. First, if there are any accusations, I am not embarrassed to get specific. For example, if the accusation is about an affair, I don't just ask, "Did you have an affair?" I ask: Did you have sex with anyone? Did you kiss anyone? Did you hold their hand? If your relationship was not physical, did you have an emotional affair by sharing intimate details with someone about your life? Do you have a relationship with someone that you haven't told your wife about? Did you buy gifts or spend money on anyone? Have you ever been accused of having an affair? I tell my clients that I hate to be surprised and that they need to tell me everything.

The second thing I do is to ask my client, "What is the opposing party not telling their attorney?" Your client may not realize it but they are in the best position to tell you about the weaknesses in the other side's case. Will the opposing party tell their attorney they are having an affair? Will they tell them they are addicted to prescription drugs? Will they tell them that they were terminated from their last job for sexual harassment? If you suspect that the other party is not being completely honest with their attorney, it is easy—and even quite enjoyable—to back them into a corner that will be quite difficult for them to crawl out of.

52.

WHEN A CLIENT OR SOMEONE ELSE IS IN JAIL

At some point in your legal career, you will have to visit the jail. Maybe your cousin got arrested for drunk driving. Maybe your client got arrested for contempt. Can you just show up at the jail, flash your bar association card, and gallop into the lock-up to save the day? No. But can you take some simple steps to make your visit to the Big House as painless as possible? Yes.

Here are some helpful hints:

1. Call ahead. Tell them you are an attorney and which inmate you are planning to visit. Ask if there are specific visiting hours. If you just show up, they could be in the middle of lunch or cell checks and there might not be staff available to help you.

2. Bring your photo identification. Most jails need proof of identity including a driver's license. Some want your bar association card as well.

3. Schedule plenty of time for your visit. You never know what the situation will be at the jail when you arrive. Believe it or not, your visit is not high on their list of priorities.

4. Don't be crabby. The jailers are not impressed that you are a lawyer. If you do not treat them in a respectful way, you may end up sitting in the waiting room a lot longer than you had planned.

5. Bring hand sanitizer. I don't care how clean the jail is, I always feel like taking a shower when I leave. Since that's not always possible, hand sanitizer has to suffice.

6. Stay focused. The people-watching opportunities at the jail are unsurpassed. On one visit, I had a quick procedural issue to notify my client about, so I spoke with her over a telephone separated by a clear window. (If you have confidential information to discuss, you should ask the jail attendant to put you in a private room, which is set aside for attorney-client meetings.) As my client and I talked on the phone, it was hard for me to concentrate

because the seventy-year-old gentleman sitting in the partition next to me was explaining to the twenty-year-old prostitute sitting next to my client how much he loved her and how glad he was about her promise to find a new career after he bonded her out. His conversation was definitely more interesting than mine.

53.

HOW TO TELL WHETHER SOMEONE IS HAVING AN AFFAIR AND WHY YOU SHOULD CARE

How many people do you know who have had an affair? I know hundreds. That's what happens when you are a divorce lawyer. And because I know hundreds, I have been able to see the patterns in what they say and what they do. The people involved in the affair think they are being clever and that no one will ever find out. Wrong.

Here is my top five list of what people in an affair say or do:

1. *"I don't love you anymore and I don't want to be married."* A previously happily married and stable individual does not just come home from work one day and say this. Think of it this way: Would you leave your current job without having another one lined up? I don't think so.

2. *"You are a terrible wife."* A previously content husband who all of the sudden starts telling his wife how awful

she is, is just making excuses to justify his decision to cheat. In his eyes, the more blame he can shift to her the better he feels.

3. *"I'm not having an affair. You're having an affair."* That's right. The person having the affair will actually accuse their innocent spouse to deflect attention away from their own bad behavior. American journalist Edward W. Howe said, "A thief believes everybody steals." Or as my dad says, "A skunk smells his own stink first."

4. They have changes in their behavior. They lose weight. They start exercising. They start tanning. They become secretive about their cell phone use and their email. They are talking on the phone at odd hours outside of your sight or ear shot.

5. They start going on business trips with a colleague of the opposite sex. This can, of course, be an appropriate business activity and completely innocent. But the gut instinct of the at-home spouse is usually right. If they are feeling that the relationship is getting emotionally or physically intimate, it probably is.

You carry a license to practice law not a badge from the morality police. So why should you care if your client's spouse is having an affair? Why should you care if your client or colleague is having an affair?

With regard to your client's spouse, your level of concern about an affair depends on what kind of case you have. If you are dealing with a divorce and you suspect that your client's spouse has expended marital funds in the furtherance of an extramarital relationship, your client has a right to know. If you have a child custody case, the judge may find that the existence of the relationship and the lies that surround it are relevant to which parent has the appropriate judgment to provide for the daily care of the children. If I suspect my client's spouse is having an affair but the spouse is refusing to admit it, I make them say under oath either through testimony or interrogatories that they are not engaged in a romantic and/or sexual relationship with a person other than their spouse. Then at least if information comes to our attention later that proves they were lying, we may have some recourse with the court.

What do you do when your client is the one having the affair? I tell my clients to end the relationship immediately.

They need to focus their energy on our case. The involvement of a third party will further complicate an already complicated situation.

So why should you care if your colleague is having an affair? An affair would be a definite red flag that all is not well in your colleague's life. Affairs involve secrecy. Don't allow yourself to get drawn into their cover-up and self-destructive behavior. That being said, your job is to work with them and not judge them. The better course is to maintain the appropriate boundaries with them so you don't become part of the drama as well.

54.

HOW TO GET YOUR CLIENT TO TELL YOU THE TRUTH

In law school, I vaguely recall a class where you were taught to communicate with your clients. But, never having had a client before, it was difficult for me to pretend to be a lawyer with a volunteer who was pretending to be my client. I would submit that instead of offering this class to you as a student, you should get a voucher that allows you to return after one year in practice.

So how do you get your client to tell you the truth—not just their truth—but the whole truth and nothing but the truth?

First, although it may sound cliché, you need to be yourself. What works for me will not necessarily work for you. I am a mother, a sister, a friend. I am fairly informal with my clients. My first question usually is: What can I help you with?

Second, you need to get your client talking. Your clients, generally, are not lawyers. They don't know what facts are important and what facts are not. If you only speak to someone for ten minutes, you are not going to learn about them and their case. Don't just ask them about the facts of the case. Make sure you find out where they grew up, what their level of education is, how many kids they have. The more you let them talk and are interested in what they are saying, the more they will talk to you. If this happens, important facts about the case will come out in unexpected places.

Third, now that they are talking, you need to stress to them the importance of telling the truth. I tell my clients flat out that I cannot help them if they don't tell me the truth. There are some clients who have the impression that they are paying you to shade the truth and get a better outcome for them by fabricating "facts." Your clients need to hear from you that you do not operate that way and that judges and juries will see through the lie. Hiding something just because they feel it will be detrimental to their case is one of the biggest mistakes they can make. Judges and juries just aren't that dumb.

I have a sign in my office that says, "It is what it is." I tell my clients that the sign means, quite simply, tell me the truth and we will deal with it together.

55.

YOU MAY BE THE ONLY SANE PERSON IN YOUR CLIENT'S LIFE

Some of your clients will reside in a far-off place called Dysfunction Junction. They don't live there alone. There are many residents including their friends and family. And here's the surprising part—they don't know they are living there. It's been my experience that the journey from normal to abnormal has been so gradual and over such a period of years that they don't even realize how out of control their lives are. They don't remember what it was like to even visit Sane Lane.

It is a fact of life that your client's family and friends will be giving advice about the case. So how can you limit the impact of the Dysfunction Junction residents as you try to obtain a good outcome for your client?

First, get to know your client. When you have a better understanding of their background and who is advising them, you will be better able to help them. You cannot undo years of psychological damage but you can identify what (or whom) their particular obstacles might be to a good outcome.

Second, be very clear about what you expect from your client, particularly in a time of emotional crisis. You cannot assume that they will act in a rational way or that they will be given accurate advice from those around them. Be specific. For example, if your client has a restraining order against him or her, tell them that *no contact* means no text messages, no driving by the house, no passing notes through mutual friends. Don't assume his or her definition of *no contact* is the court's definition. Speak in concrete terms with language that is easy to understand.

Third, expect the unexpected. If your client and those around him or her are engaged in self-destructive behavior, it will most surely bubble up somewhere in your case. You may be the only sane person in your client's life, but you have a limited ability to help, so have realistic expectations.

56.

ANYONE CAN BECOME CRAZY

Many of your clients will come to you after experiencing a significantly stressful moment in their life. They have been charged with a crime. Their business has failed. They have been accused of sexual harassment. And although they may be experiencing terrible sadness, they are able to work through it and come out on the other side. Other clients, however, will have an event occur during your representation when it seems, out of the blue, that person has gone from sad to crazy. What happened?

Here's my theory. Different people have different levels of coping skills. What would cause me stress may not cause you stress. We have all constructed defense mechanisms that protect us from stress, but sometimes and for some people when that defense is pierced or pushed, a crisis can overwhelm their coping resources. Then what happens? Let me give you an example.

There was a very dear person who was not my client but was someone I knew quite well. When she called to tell me that she had discovered that her husband was having an affair, I almost didn't recognize her voice. It was higher pitched somehow. Her speech was faster. She was working to catch her breath. She sounded very little like the person I knew. The tone of desperation was unmistakable. At that moment, I wasn't sure what she was capable of. Thankfully, she stayed on the phone with me and then agreed to meet me immediately. In talking with her about this later, here's what she said: "I now understand crimes of passion. I didn't feel like myself. I knew I shouldn't do what I wanted to do, but I still wanted to do it. I knew there would be consequences for doing it, but I just didn't care." I am so thankful that she called before taking drastic action and not after she'd already done something regrettable.

What should you, as an attorney, do if you get this phone call?

1. If you believe the person is a danger to him- or herself or others, get the person immediate professional help. This may be a circumstance where you are the only thing standing between them and a life-altering consequence. Don't be afraid to call the police.

2. Summon all of your client control skills and speak in a very concrete manner. Focus only on the matter at hand. Give them simple instructions to help draw them back from the edge. For example, instead of trying to analyze their case say, "Stop the car." This is not the time for speeches.

3. Once the situation is diffused and the person has the help they need, be sure to check back in with him or her in the next hours and days. Your call may come just at the right time.

57.

HOW TO BE INVOLVED BUT NOT OVERLY INVOLVED

An incredibly sympathetic person comes to your office with a horrible problem. You are so upset about what is going on in their life that you wake up in the middle of the night with a knot in your stomach. You can't stop thinking about the case—even at your child's baseball game or while eating dinner with your family.

Believe me when I tell you that this scenario happens to lawyers every day, in every city, in every state. When you cross the line from being involved to being overly involved, your practice and your life will suffer. How can you strike the appropriate balance between caring enough and caring too much?

First, repeat this mantra, "My client got him- or herself into this mess, and I'm here to help get him or her out." This would be important for you to remember even if you only had one client. But you don't just have one client. You have dozens, and if you agonize over every stupid thing every client is doing, you will be on a fast track to an ulcer.

Second, acknowledge that you cannot help your client if you are not clearheaded about their situation. You must remain as unemotional as possible. I tell my clients that I will not be an attorney who is jumping up and down and screaming on their behalf. In fact, when I perceive that an opposing attorney has gotten too involved, I seize upon that as an opportunity for my client, because that attorney is unable to objectively evaluate their own case.

Third, you have your own problems to deal with. Your involvement in the problems of other people can give you a very convenient opportunity to ignore your own. Don't do that. As my grandma used to say, "Tend to your knitting."

58.

MAKE SURE YOUR CLIENT HAS THE SUPPORT OF FRIENDS AND FAMILY

As a young attorney, I was surprised to see people who were desperate to hide their problems from their family and friends. Maybe their marriage was ending. Maybe they had been charged with a crime. Maybe their business was failing. For example, there are people who go through a divorce and hide that fact from their family and friends. I had a close friend of a recently divorced woman approach me and say, "I think Gertrude and Gus are having marriage problems." Her friend had no idea they were already divorced. It made me so sad for Gertrude. She was grappling with one of the saddest, most significant events in her life, and she was too embarrassed to tell anyone.

To avoid this scenario, I specifically ask my clients if they are getting the support of their family and friends and then encourage them to do so if they are reluctant. Why is this important? First, these people are a tremendous support for your client both before and after whatever the legal event might be—the divorce, the crime, or the bankruptcy.

Second, these people offer valuable advice and serve as a sounding board for the important decisions that are being made. Only when they open themselves up can they relieve some pressure and receive the help and support they need.

Third, there is life after the divorce, the crime, or the bankruptcy. My dad always says, "The only way out is through." If you're busy trying to keep a secret, you're not healing. My friend in AA says, "You're only as sick as the secrets you keep." Telling people around them about what has happened will help your clients deal with their new reality and begin the process of moving on.

59.

IS THE EXTENDED FAMILY PART OF THE PROBLEM OR PART OF THE SOLUTION?

After having spent a previous chapter telling you how important it is to have your clients share their legal difficulties with family and friends, I need to discuss what happens when they over-share and all of the sudden it feels like you are trying to satisfy a dozen clients instead of just one.

Here's how this scenario commonly starts. Your client doesn't have the money to pay your retainer so he or she relies on a family member. The person paying the bill starts calling you asking for updates on the case. Then that person accompanies your client to future appointments. That person might even come to see you without the client. This scenario is especially common when your client is a young adult but the parents are still exerting quite a bit of control over him or her.

Do you have an obligation to persons other than your client who are paying your legal fees? No. Even though other people might be paying your legal fees, your client has not waived attorney-client privilege. If the client wants you to talk with a family member, have your client sign a written statement that you have permission to talk with him or her. Absent this permission, you must explain to the family member—however well intentioned he or she might be—that you simply can't talk about the case, and if he or she has any questions they need to be asked of the client, not you.

What's the best way to deal with this problem and stop over-involvement before it starts? The best way is to deal with this issue head-on at the beginning of the case when you know someone else is paying your fees. But be prepared that you may need to reassert yourself throughout the case. For example, as you are trying to settle the case, the client's parent may be very vocal about the settlement that is being negotiated. Here's a suggestion about what you might say to the parent: "You and I both have a job to do. My job is to give your son the best legal advice I can based upon my education and my years of experience. Your job is to look out for the best interests of your child and give him the best advice you can. If I tell your son to do something, I expect him to do it. If I give him a choice, he can listen to me and listen to you and then decide for himself what is best, and then we will both support him."

Most family members are very well intentioned, but you need to be firm about your expectations for their involvement.

60.

DOES YOUR CLIENT HAVE A SAFETY PLAN?

Throughout my career—first as a prosecutor and then as an attorney in private practice—I have taken special interest in issues involving domestic violence. I prosecuted my state's first contested stalking case. I have served on the board of our local domestic violence shelter for a decade. I have friends and acquaintances who have been victims. Throughout these experiences, I have learned that domestic violence can happen to anyone.

If you have a client or a friend or a family member who is involved in a relationship that is breaking up, I encourage you to ask two questions. The first question is: "Do you feel safe?"

They may look at you in surprise. So why would you ask this? Because experts know that the most dangerous time for someone in a relationship is when he or she tries to leave. The first two weeks following the breakup are especially dangerous. Encourage your clients to listen to that little voice inside of them that might be indicating that danger is possible. It doesn't matter if the other person has never laid a hand on them before. If your client, friend, or family member is pregnant, pay special attention. The second leading cause of death for pregnant women, right behind pregnancy-related health complications, is homicide.

The second question is this: "Do you have a safety plan?" A safety plan is created before a crisis arises. It insures that if something goes wrong and she feels threatened, she has a safe place to go. Wherever she's going, she's talked with them ahead of time, and they are aware she might be coming. The plan is shared with you, as her attorney, and only her most trusted loved ones.

Ignoring this problem won't make it go away. Family and relationship violence is a reality, so do what you can to protect your clients and loved ones.

SECTION VII:

BUILDING A CASE AND PREPARING FOR TRIAL

Building a case and preparing for trial requires attention to detail and plenty of time spent at your desk. It may not be exciting, but it is absolutely necessary for you to put in this time to achieve the best results for your client.

61.

MAKE SURE YOU ARE SUING AND SERVING THE RIGHT PARTY

I think it's safe to say that I am not a civil procedure genius. The book of my state's court rules is my constant companion. But it doesn't take a genius to know this: if a lawyer doesn't sue the right party and serve the right party, the plaintiff is in trouble.

In a world of parent companies, subsidiaries, and all sorts of related business entities, naming the right party may be easier said than done. So what do plaintiff's attorneys do? They name every possible party and then just dismiss them out later if they end up having little or no relationship to the case. How do defense attorneys respond to this? They complain that the plaintiff's attorneys are wasting their time and should have done their research before filing their case.

Once you have sued the right parties, you need to serve the right parties. Consequences of failing to serve the right party at the appropriate location within the time frame required by your jurisdiction can be disastrous if you're the plaintiff's attorney. If you are serving a corporation, check and double-check with the office of the Secretary of State in your jurisdiction to find out who their registered agent is. Most of the information is available online.

Here's a common scenario if you represent the defendant. A partner comes into your office, throws a petition on your desk and says, "The Smith Corp. was served with this lawsuit on the first day of this month. Our answer needs to be filed in twenty days." Should your next step be to prepare the answer? No. Your next step is to make sure that the correct party was served in the time allowed by your jurisdiction. If the process server walked in and gave the petition to the receptionist and not the corporate officer or registered agent, you may be filing a motion to dismiss for insufficiency of service of process instead of an answer.

You need to pay attention to the details. If you are the plaintiff, you can make sure that your case gets off to a clean start. If you are a defendant, you may be able to stop the case before it even begins.

62.

LOOK AT THE JURY INSTRUCTIONS TO PREPARE YOUR CASE

I am not a big fan of cutting corners because it usually has bad results. This is especially true when it comes to legal research. Research takes time. One bit of information leads to another that leads to another. You check and recheck. Cutting corners is dangerous. If something seems too easy, you probably don't understand the problem. But there is a resource out there that makes everything seem clear. This resource is written in plain language that is easy to understand. It can give focus to your research or assist in the preparation of your petition. The resource I am referring to are the standard jury instructions from your jurisdiction. You can find them online and your law office will also have them in book form.

Let me give you a couple of examples of when to use them:

• You have been asked to research whether an employer has a cause of action against their former employee who is wooing their clients away. Go to the jury instructions. They will be organized into contracts, torts, and so on. By reviewing the jury instructions, you can find out what causes of action may be available. You know what you would have to prove to a jury. You then review the facts of your case to decide if the employer has met the requirements. An added bonus is that the jury instructions are often annotated which means that they reference court cases which will explain the instruction further.

- You have been asked to prepare a petition for a case. You have a sample petition from another case and maybe even a form from your state bar. But how do you make sure you have covered the bases and alleged each element of your cause of action? You double check with the jury instructions. The instructions will also give you guidance about the different types of damages that may apply to your case.

The lesson is that jury instructions aren't just for juries anymore. Think of them like a road map. They show you where you need to go and, if you study them, you just may find the shortest route.

63.

DON'T WAIT FOR SOMEONE TO GIVE YOU INFORMATION

Wouldn't it be nice if there was an Information Fairy that tucked financial affidavits, tax returns, and interrogatory responses under your desk each night? As much as we all want to believe this fairy exists, we can't wait until the night before the trial to get to work. We need accurate and complete facts and documents to effectively represent our clients.

This process starts after your client walks out the door from the initial interview. You and your assistant should meet to discuss the dates involved in the case including discovery deadlines and what type of information you need and when. What this information will be is, of course, dependent on what type of case you have. Be prepared to have your client sign a release or authorization that allows people to provide you with the information you want.

In addition to interrogatories, consider requiring the other party to produce the following: medical and counseling records, job applications, substance abuse evaluations, and credit reports. Also consider using a subpoena to get documents directly from third parties including personnel documents from a party's employer. Don't underestimate the value of a court record search and basic Internet search to see if anything interesting pops up.

For future reference, compile a sample file just for interrogatories and requests for production prepared by you (or someone else) that you thought were particularly helpful or well-crafted. Check with your state bar association to see if they have a practice manual for the area of law in which you are working. In addition to forms for a variety of pleadings, it may also include suggestions for discovery.

Make sure you utilize your client to supply documentation. Whatever you do, don't wait until the last minute. Just because you are in a hurry, doesn't mean that a clerk in an office somewhere is going to feel your same sense of urgency.

64.

PREPARE FOR DEPOSITIONS

Depositions are an important part of your case. In a deposition, an attorney asks questions and a witness gives sworn answers. Depositions can be taken for discovery purposes or for evidentiary purposes. In discovery depositions, the questions can cover a wide range of topics. As long as the questions are reasonably calculated to lead to relevant evidence, they can be asked even if the responses ultimately may not be admissible at the trial. In evidentiary depositions, persons who may not be available at the time of the trial are subject to both direct and cross-examination. In both discovery and evidentiary depositions, the attorney may object to a line of questioning, and a judge will later determine what is admissible.

If your client is being deposed, you should meet with him ahead of time and practice. Go over what the deposition will be like. Read (and follow) Chapter 75 about how to prepare your witness. The wrong answer in a deposition can damage—or sometimes even completely sink—your entire case. It's your job to make sure that you have done what you can to get them ready. Make sure they have reviewed their reports and previous statements.

If you are asking the questions, write out a list of questions so you don't forget to cover something. You will add or subtract from those questions depending on the witnesses' answers, but having at least an outline will help you to focus and stay organized. Know what you have to prove or disprove in the case, and keep that in mind when you are fashioning your questions.

Also anticipate the legal issues in the case and do some research. If you know that the other side is going to try to ask questions about a topic that would be inadmissible, have some case law to back you up.

Finally, when the court reporter sends you a copy of the transcript, review it carefully. I had a case involving libel and the court reporter used the word "liable" instead, so the deposition was corrected. It is a humbling experience to read your first several depositions. The number of times you will say "Um" or "Okay" is especially embarrassing, so learn from your mistakes and be even more prepared next time.

65.

GIVE MEDIATION A TRY

Mediation is becoming more and more popular. In some jurisdictions, it's more than popular—it's mandatory. If you are mediating by choice or by order, you need to make the best use of this opportunity as you possibly can. Here are two words for a successful mediation—preparation and participation.

With regard to preparation, some attorneys say that the key to a successful mediation is the opportunity to submit a mediation brief in advance of the date and time set for the mediation. It's a win-win situation. The mediator likes the opportunity to consider the complex issues involved in the case prior to the date and time set for mediation. You like the opportunity to convince the mediator that the other side's case isn't as strong as they think it is. Write a persuasive factual statement followed by detailed legal research and argument. You have to give the mediator the ammunition to walk into the room of the opposing party and help them to understand that they are taking a huge risk just by choosing to continue with the case. If pre-submission is not an option, then submit the brief on the day of the mediation.

You also need to prepare your client. If you believe the mediator may give them an opportunity to make a statement at the beginning of the mediation, you need to make sure they are ready. Let the other side see what a great witness they will be. Also discuss with your client a range of settlement possibilities in advance to make the best use of your time at the mediation.

Being an active participant at the mediation is essential. Listen carefully. Communicate clearly. Talk to and counsel your client. Even if the mediation is turning out to be a waste of time, you should still glean what you can from the other side's case. Are there any new facts or twists on legal arguments that you will need to follow up on? Even if you don't get the case settled, you can still get some insight into what you're facing.

66.

HOW YOU KNOW WHEN YOU HAVE A GOOD SETTLEMENT

The title of this chapter sounds like the beginning of lawyer joke, but it's not. The way you know if you have a good settlement is if both sides of the case are equally unhappy. That's not a typo. I wrote *unhappy*. Both parties being a little dissatisfied means that each party gave a little in order to get the case settled. In order to avoid the risk and uncertainty that comes with a trial, they both walked away.

But would it be so bad if your client was thrilled with the outcome and the other side was miserable? In most situations, no. But in some situations it can cause years of heartache. If the parties have an ongoing relationship because of children or for some other reason, the other party may harbor the resentment of getting the short end of the stick forever. Generally, if a settlement offer is that lopsided, the party will simply take their chances in court.

There are also times when you disagree with your client's decision to settle. You believe that making a deal is worse than rolling the dice with a judge or jury. It might help to put yourself in your client's shoes. Maybe he or she doesn't want to spend any more money on attorney fees. Maybe they are just plain tired of it. Even though you may be fairly confident that if you went to court that you could get more than what you are agreeing to, you need to accept and support the decision. Hopefully, if you have communicated with your client throughout the case, these situations will be few and far between.

Occasionally, your client will agree to settle and then get cold feet prior to the final documents being filed. He or she may call you and try to renegotiate some of the terms to which he or she previously agreed. This is a time when you need to summon all of your client control skills. Unless some significant and unforeseen circumstance has occurred, you need to state that the case has been settled. Try to remind the client about the reasons the settlement was reached in the first place. Most times, the client is just looking for a little reassurance. However, if the client insists on backing out, you should consider withdrawing from the case. The opposing counsel was relying on your representation that the case was settled. Your professional credibility could be seriously damaged if you break your word.

67.

HOPE FOR THE BEST BUT PREPARE FOR AND EXPECT THE WORST

This chapter could also be called "Never let your guard down."

Occasionally, a client will come in your office and declare, "I think this case is pretty straight forward," or "I think this case should be easy for you." What the client is really trying to say is, "I don't want to spend much on attorney fees." Although, in the end, the prediction may be completely accurate, you cannot let blind optimism get in the way of obtaining a sufficient retainer and appropriately preparing your case.

Is it a waste of time to hope for the best? Absolutely not. For the most part, I consider each case a clean slate regardless of the history the other attorney and I share. I sincerely hope that we will all work hard and that our clients will be reasonable. However, if you are too busy hoping for the best, you may be neglecting to adequately prepare your case.

If you keep a positive attitude but set your naïveté aside, how do you prepare for the worst?

1. Do the appropriate discovery. It is easy to put things off because the case is going so well and you are just sure that things will work out without you having to go through all of the formalities. Take the time to send the interrogatories or subpoena the documents you need.

2. Prepare a witness list and make sure they are available for your hearing or trial date. They can always cross the date off later if you get things settled.

3. Prepare an exhibit list and make sure you have everything you need or at least can put your hands on it at the last minute if necessary.

4. Don't wait until the last minute to call the other attorney and see how far you are apart on settlement.

5. Beware of the attorney who doesn't call you back or answer your letters. He or she may not want to share what their strategy is and could be preparing for a gotcha moment.

One final thought. There is a constant push and pull between your client's ability to pay for your fees and your need to spend adequate time preparing. Regardless of how your client hopes the case may unfold, you should prepare them for the possibility of an expensive outcome.

68.

YOUR PRETRIAL SETTLEMENT DISCUSSION WITH YOUR CLIENT

Every attorney has had this happen. You spend hours and hours of your client's money getting ready for trial. The witnesses have been subpoenaed. Your exhibits have been marked. Then, on the morning of trial, the case gets settled on the courthouse steps or in the judge's chambers. Even though a settlement is usually a good thing, it is frustrating when a case settles on the morning of trial and the same result could have been achieved several weeks prior, thereby avoiding a great deal of expense and stress.

Is it possible to avoid this scenario 100 percent of time? No, because even the most confident clients get cold feet on the morning of trial. But here's a suggestion for avoiding it most of the time—a pretrial settlement meeting with your client.

This meeting involves putting everything on the table with your client. This doesn't happen the morning of trial; it happens several weeks prior to trial, using all of the information you have gathered to that point. It mostly likely occurs before you have had serious settlement negotiations with opposing counsel. You and your client have a frank discussion about the strengths and weaknesses of the case, the cost of trial preparation, and the minimum and maximum your client can expect from the judge or jury. You then work with your client to arrive at your final, last offer. Both you and your client will have an understanding of what it will take to get the case settled, and it gives you the freedom to approach opposing counsel and start negotiating.

If you feel your client is taking an unreasonable position with regard to settlement, put the details of your meeting in writing. That way, if the case settles on the courthouse steps, it will be difficult for your client to explain that his or her money was wasted on trial preparation.

SECTION VIII:

SUCCESS IN THE COURTROOM

Successful attorneys display three positive qualities to a judge or jury at all times—sincerity, competence, and respect. Sincerity means that you can be yourself in the courtroom while putting forth a good faith argument on behalf of your client. Competence means that you know the law and the facts, and you have the ability to convey them in a succinct and orderly fashion. Respect means that you show deference to the jury, the judge, opposing counsel, the parties, the witnesses, and all court personnel.

69.

DON'T THROW A FIT IN COURT

For most new attorneys, appearing in court is a scary thing. You may be so frightened of the judge that you can barely summon the courage to make eye contact with him or her. But as you get more experienced, the terror wears off and your deference to the court may also diminish. That's when your behavior can get you into trouble. Some attorneys will even throw fits.

I've seen attorneys throw papers. Storm out. Make faces. Complain softly. Complain loudly. If the under-five crowd understands that throwing a fit has consequences, can't an attorney grasp that concept as well? How can we expect our clients to show respect for our system of justice if we act like children in the courtroom?

Attorneys throw fits for three primary reasons. First, they are trying to divert attention from their own failures or omissions. If they receive an adverse ruling that their client was surprised by or unprepared for, the attorney will act as if the outcome was some outrageous event that was so unexpected that the only possible reaction is shock and disgust.

Second, attorneys get frustrated and tired. There are long days in the courtroom and sometimes you get to the point that you've forgotten what you're fighting for. Hopefully, if a judge sees that your temperature is rising after a long day, he or she may give everyone an opportunity for a short break.

Third, the judge has made the wrong decision or has made a mistake. But guess what? Judges are human, and that does not give you permission to show disrespect to the court. Any good coach will tell you that you need to play through the bad calls.

Judges understand that attorneys may be disappointed by the rulings. Most will even understand if occasionally a mild reaction is noticeable. However, if the court is offended enough by how an attorney is behaving, a trip to the time-out chair—a.k.a. jail—may be in their future.

70.

TREAT THE OTHER ATTORNEY'S CLIENT WITH RESPECT

You have a definite opinion about the opposing parties in the case. You know all of their dirty secrets. You know how mean they've been. You know how dishonest they have been. Why should you make nice with them? Because it is important to our system of justice, that's why. Now I'm not suggesting that you exchange holiday cards or take a pottery class together. What I am suggesting is that your behavior toward the opposing party colors their perception about whether they have been treated fairly by the court system.

Here's an example of what happens when the line between professional and personal gets crossed. I had a client who had been divorced for several years. I did not represent him in the original divorce, but he came to me to discuss a possible modification. He complained to me that his ex-wife's attorney hated him. I assured him that she did not hate him and was just zealously representing her client. When we finally got to court, I understood why my client felt that way. I was surprised that the other attorney seethed when my client walked in the room. She questioned him in a hostile fashion about matters not relevant to the proceeding. There was a personal element to her representation that both puzzled and troubled me. For my client, his feeling that the other attorney was out to get him turned the courtroom into a place for personal vendettas rather than equity.

My husband has been a judge for over a decade. He makes a diligent effort to treat everyone in his courtroom with an even hand. He believes that if a criminal defendant or the parties to a lawsuit feel that the judge is being unfair or is out to get them, they will not focus on changing the behavior that got them to court in the first place.

A final thought on this. You may want to warn your client that the mere fact that you treat the other party with respect and courtesy does not mean that you have crossed over to the Dark Side. It's the exact opposite. By being positive and fair, you are fighting more effectively for your client.

71.

FIND A NICE JUDGE YOU CAN TALK TO

I was raised with a healthy respect for authority figures and so, even as an adult, I cannot call teachers or doctors by their first names. Imagine how I felt appearing in front of a judge for the first time. For many attorneys just starting out, judges can be pretty intimidating. After all, they are the all-knowing and all-powerful decision makers. When they are on the bench, they are serious, no nonsense folks.

But there is another side to judges. They were once lawyers, too. Although my husband loves his job as a judge, there are days that he misses the comradery that he felt as a prosecutor. Judges love to talk about their experiences and their former practice and also to hear about yours. They have families, children, interests, and hobbies.

It is true that some judges are friendlier than others. Some are more helpful than others. I believe all of them have a keen interest in helping young attorneys become better practitioners. After a case is resolved, if you feel like the judge would be receptive to it, ask him or her to critique how you did. You're not asking for a pat on the back. You are asking for an honest opinion, so brace yourself for what you might hear. If he or she is willing to do this, the judge can offer incredibly helpful advice to improve your trial practice. This is not a chance for you to reargue your case. It's a chance for you to hear what your performance looked like from the other side of the bench.

72.

RESEARCH YOUR JUDGE

New attorneys or attorneys practicing in a new district or jurisdiction are at a definite disadvantage when it comes to predicting what a judge might do. Experienced attorneys know which judges are more or less sympathetic to different types of clients. They know the type of law the judge practiced before coming to the bench. They know which judges have a very formal courtroom and which are more relaxed. They know which judge will start without you if you are a minute late for the hearing.

Early in my practice, I represented a criminal defendant in a drunk-driving case. When we appeared in front of the judge for sentencing, my client was not as forthright as what I wish he had been when the judge asked him how much he had to drink on the night in question. The judge gave him a harsher sentence than even the prosecutor was recommending. For this judge, it wasn't enough that he was pleading guilty. The judge wanted to know that my client was actually taking responsibility and ownership for what he had done.

Several weeks later, I was asked by a fellow attorney about a client who was to appear in front of this same judge for a guilty plea on a sexual abuse charge. I instructed him, "Your client must admit his guilt without qualification and be able to explain what he did without hesitation. If he doesn't, the judge will not follow the plea agreement." So what happened? Either the lawyer didn't take my advice or his client didn't take his advice. The client hemmed and hawed about what he did or didn't do, and the judge sent him to jail right on the spot.

The lesson: So much of the outcome of a case is beyond your control. Finding out what you can about the judge's background and courtroom is just one more way to represent your client in the most efficient and effective way possible.

73.

BE EXTREMELY CAREFUL WITH EX PARTE COMMUNICATIONS

One of the fastest ways for you to lose your reputation in the legal community is to go behind someone's back with a judge. Most attorneys and judges are very conscientious about not engaging in ex parte communication. Its occurrence is more by accident than by design. It's more a reflection of being just a little too familiar with a judge.

When you are right out of law school, you probably don't know many judges and the contact you have with them is limited and formal. But the longer you practice the more likely it is that someone you went to law school with or spent considerable time with is going to end up on the bench. In public, you have to keep this relationship as professional as possible. It is a poor reflection on our system if the party on the other side of the case feels like you have an unfair advantage because of your relationship with the judge. It goes without saying that when you are alone with the judge in a social setting, you are absolutely forbidden from talking about the case.

This can be a very sticky situation. When I need to talk to a judge about a case, even if it's just to give a required update on settlement, I always get permission from the other attorney and offer to have a conference call if he or she would prefer. But sometimes a conversation happens without advance notice. A common scenario is that you are talking to the judge about Case A, and he or she also asks about Case B. The attorney for Case B is not there, and so you and the judge need to be careful that your comments are limited to the most basic and brief update without any attempt at argument or persuasion. But even that little contact can be seen as problematic by the absent attorney.

Even more troublesome are ex parte orders. It's one thing to have a conversation with a judge without the other attorney. It is quite another to obtain an order on a contested matter with one party absent. Even if it is technically allowable, you are walking through a mine field if you try to do this. You don't know what your client is not telling you, and shortcuts may generate more litigation than a full and fair hearing with all parties present.

74.

DO THESE THINGS BEFORE YOU ASK THE JUDGE FOR A SIGNATURE

Despite how it is portrayed in television and movies, much of what we do as lawyers is desk work that involves uncontested, unglamorous legal matters. The parties have agreed to the outcome or a formality needs to be complied with. Although you need a judge's signature, the judge really doesn't want or need to have much more involvement than that. Here are some suggestions to make your time with the judge as efficient and productive as possible:

1. Start by finding out if the court has a specific time period where these types of orders can be signed. Some jurisdictions prefer that you appear in front of a specific judge at a specific time to avoid all of the judges being interrupted throughout the day. If no such time period has been set aside, then find out if a judge is available and when would be the most convenient time to stop by.

2. If needed, get permission from the other side to the talk to the judge.

3. Dress appropriately even though you are not officially appearing in court.

4. When you get to the courthouse, retrieve the court file from the clerk of court. Some judges like to flip through it before signing the order.

5. Have a prepared order. Don't show up and expect the judge to prepare the order in your case. If you need something set for hearing, prepare an order with blanks for the date and time. If there are multiple potential options of how to proceed, I prepare two orders and let the judge decide which he or she would like to sign.

6. Set aside enough time. Bring extra work to keep you busy if the judge is unexpectedly engaged or you have to wait your turn.

7. If you have never met the judge before, be sure to introduce yourself and let him or her know the name of your law firm.

75.

HOW TO GET YOUR WITNESS READY FOR COURT

Because attorneys are comfortable in court, they forget how uncomfortable everyone else is. For most of your clients and their witnesses, the thought of testifying in a court proceeding is scary. They will lose sleep over it. Their fear may even impact their ability to focus and recall accurately the events in question. You may never be able to alleviate all their fears but by preparing them for what they might expect, they may rest a little easier.

Start by telling your client and each witness that the most important thing for them to do is to tell the truth. That may seem obvious to you but the concept is surprisingly difficult for some. I tell my client and the witnesses that it is not their job to figure out what impact their testimony will have on the outcome of the case. They just need to tell the facts as they know them. It's especially fun when the opposing attorney asks my witness, "Did the lawyer talk to you before the hearing today?" And my witness responds, "Yes, and she told me to tell the truth."

Second, tell them to answer only the questions they are asked. If a question calls for a yes-or-no answer, then answer "yes" or "no" or "I can't answer yes or no because..." They should not volunteer information or get chatty.

Third, tell them not to guess. If they don't know something or can't recall, then that is what they need to say. If they aren't sure what the lawyer means, they shouldn't guess at what he means. Instead, they should ask for clarification.

Fourth, tell them they need to speak loudly enough for everyone to hear them. They cannot nod or shake their head for an answer, they need to verbally answer yes or no. If they are speaking too quickly or answering before the lawyer is done asking the question, the court reporter will not be happy with them.

Finally, tell them not to let anyone put words in their mouth. They need to listen carefully to the questions and if something is not stated correctly, they need to speak up. This is their testimony, and it needs to accurately reflect what they know.

76.

YOU AND YOUR CLIENT SHOULD DRESS APPROPRIATELY FOR COURT

A defendant appearing on a drunk-driving charge showed up in court for his guilty plea wearing a shirt that said, "I don't have a drinking problem. I drink. I get drunk. I fall down. No problem." That is a true story. The judge sent the man home and made him change his shirt. Was the judge expecting him to appear in court in formal evening attire? No. But he was expecting that he would come wearing something that showed the proper level of respect for the court and the proceeding.

You cannot assume that your clients have an appropriate understanding of courtroom expectations, so you need to have a discussion with them about how they will dress for court. I tell my clients to wear what they would if they were going to church or to meet their significant other's parents for the first time. Be dressed up, but comfortable.

Minimal jewelry. No tee shirts. No jeans. Don't chew gum. The court does not need to see cleavage or tattoos. I know this sounds crazy, but you may even need to tell your client to bathe before court. It's better coming from you than the judge.

Even though you want your clients to be presentable, don't try to turn them into someone they're not. If your client has never worn a suit but you force him to wear one in court, the judge or jury may mistake his discomfort for dishonesty. The better course is to let him be himself. While still being sufficiently dressy, he needs to be comfortable enough to focus on the case.

For attorneys, call me old-fashioned, but men should wear a coat and tie. Women may have a little more flexibility but you still need to be dressy. A basic suit is always a safe choice.

77.

HOW TO PRESENT YOUR CASE TO THE JUDGE

Not all cases are tried to a jury. In fact, most cases are tried in front of a judge. What do you think will impress the judge the most? Your adorable suit? Your wealthy client? Your fancy smart phone? No. What will impress the judge is your ability to present your case in an organized and logical manner that demonstrates you have an understanding of the facts and of the law.

So what does it take to be organized? One word: preparation. Here are a few suggestions on how to be best prepared:

1. Start with a witness list. Compile a list of all of the possible people who may be needed at the trial. As the trial gets closer, spend time talking with them. They may be able to provide you information you didn't even know they had. Make sure that they are aware of the date, time, and place of the hearing. Get

them a subpoena if necessary. Try to schedule them in a way that uses the court's time most efficiently. The judge does not want to wait twenty minutes if your witness has not arrived yet.

2. Make an exhibit list. Think through the documents that you need to prepare or obtain. Cross reference your exhibit list to the witness list. Which exhibits will you use with each witness? Do you have the appropriate witness in order to admit the exhibit? Before the hearing starts, give this list to the judge and to opposing counsel.

3. Write out your witness questions. This will organize your thoughts and will serve as a guide to you as you present your case. You of course will be asking many additional questions based upon the testimony and evidence at the hearing, but there may be questions that you must not forget to ask. It's not unusual that in the hustle and bustle of a trial that an attorney will let one of those "must-ask" questions go unasked. Having at least some questions prepared allows you to focus on the testimony as it comes in without leaving out anything important.

So what does it take to present your case in a logical way? One word, same word: preparation. You need to know your case well enough that your witnesses and exhibits serve a purpose in advancing your case. You need to know your facts well enough that you can apply them to existing law. Do your research and then put it in a format that you can submit to the judge and opposing counsel. Different jurisdictions may call this document a Trial Brief or Trial Statement. Whatever they call it, take time to do a good one. I like to include vital information on both my client and the other party. What is their date of birth, do they have children, where do they work, what is the current status of their health. I include relevant statutes and case law. I also include a requested disposition and include exactly what I would like the ruling to say. One of my happiest moments as a lawyer is when I read a court's order that has taken language from my brief verbatim and simply plopped it in the order.

78.

TIPS FOR PICKING A JURY

Even though prospective jurors are not to form an opinion on the case until they have heard all of the evidence, many attorneys will agree with this statement: cases can be won or lost in jury selection. That's why some firms will hire psychologists or jury consultants or even mock jurors in order to make sure that their client has the advantage. It may take years (that's right, years) for you to feel comfortable in jury selection, but here are few thoughts and suggestions:

1. Jury selection gives the jury an opportunity to get to know you but it is not an opportunity to talk about yourself and your accomplishments. To be successful, you need to possess the sincere desire to pick an impartial jury for your client. You can't fake sincerity. When you treat the jurors with respect, they are more likely to answer openly and honestly.

2. Jury selection gives you an opportunity to get to know the jury. You need to uncover if a prospective juror's attitudes and experiences may have an impact on your case. That's really the bottom line. If you are representing a plaintiff in a slip-and-fall case, don't you want to find out if any of the prospective jurors have been landlords or store owners? But it's not enough to just get an answer to a simple question. You have to be prepared to engage in a discussion with them about their experiences. In most cases, the entire prospective jury panel will be listening to your conversation with each juror, so try to use that dialogue as a chance to educate the jury about the theory of your case without crossing the line into objectionable argument.

3. How do you get the jurors to put themselves into the role of finders of the facts? Here's a suggestion for a series of questions:

   • If you are a juror in this case, you will be the judge of the facts. Have you ever been a judge or a referee?

- Have you ever judged a baking contest, refereed a soccer game, or umpired a baseball game?

- Do you think the people who were participating were expecting you to be fair and impartial?

- Do you think it's important to call the strike zone the same for everyone?

- What qualities should my client be looking for in a judge of the facts?

4. Talk about the credibility of witnesses. You need to make sure your jurors are comfortable with sorting through the various versions of the story that will be presented. The reality is that memory is not always reliable. Divergent views can bring divergent testimony. A person's interest in the case can influence their perceptions of the events.

5. If you have a difficult concept, explain it and then ask if that explanation makes sense. Instead of saying, "What does *reasonable doubt* mean to you?" say, "The judge may tell you that if you are firmly convinced then you do not have a reasonable doubt. Would you

agree that there is a difference between 'beyond a reasonable doubt' and 'beyond all doubt'? Does that make sense to you?"

Here's the reality. Picking a jury is like learning to swim. You can't learn to do it by reading a book—you have to jump in. But find some comfort in the fact that the more you do it, the better you'll get.

79.

CROSS-EXAMINATION— YOU'RE NO PERRY MASON

Every attorney dreams of the Perry Mason moment. That moment when the opposing party collapses under your amazing cross-examination. The judge immediately declares your client the victor, and the jury is summarily dismissed. Every attorney dreams about it because it rarely, if ever, happens. Why doesn't it happen? Because cross-examination is one of the most difficult things a lawyer does.

Why is it so hard? Because you are trying to get information from someone who doesn't want to give it to you. In fact, the person on the stand would like the court to hear information that will damage your case. In this situation and with this witness, your measure of success is not total victory. Your measure of success is actually something much less. Your goal is to make a few important points and be done. Here's how.

1. As you prepare questions in advance, ask yourself, "What do I need to accomplish with this witness?" "How does this question help me prove my case?" How you ask your questions is a tactic; why you ask your questions is a strategy.

2. Listen carefully to the direct examination. Did the testimony come in as you thought it would? If not, what are the points you want to make?

3. Start off by being positive. Have the witness affirm everything that you know is not a fight. Take baby steps toward your major points. Don't just come right out and ask the ultimate question. Lead the witness in that direction little by little. Then, at the end, they will look foolish for disagreeing with you.

4. You shouldn't ask questions that you don't already know the answers to. You should be using leading questions and rarely, if ever, start a question with the word "Why." Think of it this way—sometimes the point of cross-examination is not to get answers to questions—sometimes the point is to state your case to the judge or the jury in the guise of a

question. It's more about your question than the witness's answer.

5. Be persistent. If the witness is trying to avoid answering your question, keep asking. It may raise an "Ask and answered" objection from opposing counsel, but don't let the witness take control by his or her refusal to answer.

6. Keep your emotions in check. The general rule is to show little or no emotion. Juries and judges don't like an obnoxious attorney, with one rare exception. The exception is when the witness gives you a ticket to do it. How does the witness do this? By being unusually snotty, arrogant, deceitful, or annoying. If you feel like the jury wants you to be more assertive, a hint of well-placed sarcasm or a bit of mild disgust on your part will score a few points and make you look like the good guy. But it's a risky move, because if you're wrong, you look like the jerk.

80.

KNOW WHEN TO SIT DOWN AND SHUT UP

When I went back for my twenty-year high school reunion, one of my classmates was not the least bit surprised that I was an attorney. As he fondly remembered, "You always did like to argue." The legal profession is full of people like me. You can argue any side of any issue for any length of time. There are moments, however, when you need to stop arguing.

One such moment came early in my career. I was prosecuting criminal cases and was arguing an issue involving the state's access to the defendant's medical records. I felt like every time the defense attorney made an argument, that I needed to respond to it. Finally, the judge said, "Ms. Thalacker, you are winning. I don't think you should say anything else." It was a great lesson, and over the years I have tried to recognize those times when continuing to speak can only hurt my case. But how do you know when less is more?

First, look to the judge and the jury for clues. They may be giving you verbal or nonverbal cues that continued testimony or argument is not necessary or will actually hurt you. For example, there are times in a criminal case when everyone in the courtroom knows that the state's case is so bad that the defendant shouldn't testify. His testimony is the only way he will be convicted.

Second, if you know your case, you should be able to boil it down and explain it succinctly to a judge or jury. Brevity is closely related to clarity. If the other attorney is rambling on and on, you get the feeling that he or she doesn't really know what the main point is.

Third, the longer you practice, the better able you are to get to the heart of the matter. You have conquered your own internal fears that you are missing the issues. As you get more experienced, you do your work faster. You know what the points are. You know what's persuasive. It's a process of being able to identify and direct your questions and argument to the essential portion of the case.

81.

MAKE YOUR RECORD
FOR APPEAL

I'm a golfer who makes liberal use of mulligans. A mulligan is a "do-over." A chance to erase your last shot and try again. Wouldn't it be nice to get a few mulligans in your law practice? But alas, the legal world is not a golf course, and when your case is on appeal, you can't scurry back into court and tee up another exhibit. You are stuck with your record, so make it a good one.

It's helpful to explain this concept to your client before—not after—the trial. Make sure they know that they get one bite at the apple. This is his or her one chance to talk to the judge and show him or her what you have. It's now or never.

When in court, you need to be organized enough to make sure the exhibits you have offered are actually admitted into evidence by the judge. You also need to preserve your issues for appeal. If the issue wasn't presented to the judge or the objection wasn't made at the trial, it's difficult, if not impossible, to argue it on appeal. If you do make an objection and the reason for the judge's ruling on it is unclear, try to get the judge to explain his or her rationale, but do this in a polite and deferential way. Judges don't like to have their rulings questioned, and they are definitely better at asking questions than answering them.

You should also be familiar with your jurisdiction's procedure for making an offer of proof. The offer is a presentation of evidence at the trial court level that will not be considered by the trial court but that may be considered by the appeals court. In other words, it's a way for you to let the appellate court know what the evidence would have been if you had been allowed to present it.

A word of warning. Most attorneys right out of law school are more familiar with appeals than they are with trial work. Evidence does not magically appear in the appellate record. You need to put it there, so pay attention to your burden of proof and the elements of your case, and then present the testimony, issues, argument, and objections that will preserve them for appeal.

82.

APPEALS ARE A DIFFERENT ANIMAL

It is your case. You spent hours preparing. You had countless meetings (and headaches) with your client and the witnesses. You cross-examined the opposing party. You did the research for the trial brief. You prepared the post-trial motions. No one knows the case better than you. But are you the best person to do the appeal? Before you make a decision, ask yourself these questions:

1. Can you follow directions? Whichever jurisdiction you are in, I can guarantee that there are pages and pages of directions in the rules of appellate procedure. The rules deal with everything from the width of your margins to the color of your paper. Some jurisdictions are lenient when a defect is brought to their attention. Other jurisdictions have a zero-tolerance policy and will kick your documents right back to

you. Does this sound enjoyable or tedious? If it sounds enjoyable, keep reading.

2.   Do you feel ready for the oral argument? Depending on your jurisdiction, you may be required to participate in an oral argument. Does that possibility excite you or make you nauseous? If you are excited by the thought of being peppered with questions by several people in robes, keep reading.

3.   Do you have an attorney in your office who has both the experience and the time to help you? Be sure to clear it with him or her before taking on an appeal, and also keep his or her assistant in the loop.

4.   Is it in your client's best interests for you to handle the appeal? Be honest with your client about your level of appellate experience. If they still want you to handle it and you have answered in the affirmative to the first three questions, you might want to give it a try.

83.

GETTING MORE
TIME IN COURT

If you want to be a trial attorney, there are certain very well-established paths you can choose. Government work at a prosecutor's office or public defender's office is where many notable trial attorneys have begun their careers. You may be overworked and underpaid, but your contribution to the community and the courtroom experience you gain makes it well worth your while.

It may not be as easy for attorneys in private practice to get the courtroom experience they need. Civil cases take years to make it to court, and clients don't want to take a chance on an inexperienced litigator. If you are working at a private law firm and would like to see the inside of a courtroom prior to your partnership vote, here are a few suggestions:

1. Take on pro bono cases that are more likely to get you into court.

2. Represent defendants in criminal matters.

3. Make requests to second-chair more experienced attorneys from your firm during their trials. In a complex civil litigation case, it would be rare to only have one attorney at counsel table. The attorney may even let you examine a witness or two.

4. Participate in arbitration proceedings as often as you can. Many jurisdictions have mandatory arbitration for cases with smaller values. Although it is different than a courtroom, you will still get the experience of preparing your case and presenting your witnesses and evidence.

5. Attend a hands-on legal education seminar that improves your trial advocacy skills.

6. Find out if there is a chapter of the *American Inns of Court* (AIC) in your area and submit an application. One of their goals is to help less experienced attorneys become more effective advocates and counselors. It would be a great opportunity for you to meet distinguished members of the bar and bench in a less formal setting.

84.

HAVE A SINCERE
APPRECIATION FOR
COURT PERSONNEL

This may come as a complete shock to you but many lawyers have inflated views of themselves. Contrary to their firmly held belief, however, the court system is not in orbit around them, and the nonlawyers in the court system are not employed to respond to their every whim. Here's another shock: the nonlawyers often have more knowledge about what you need to do in your case than you do.

As a new practitioner, I want you to admit that you have little understanding of the nuts and bolts of how the courthouse actually functions. Now what do you do to remedy that? Here are some suggestions to increase your knowledge and also utilize the expertise of the rest of the participants in the court system:

1. Introduce yourself to the people in the courthouse offices. If you don't have a colleague who will do

this, go yourself. Be friendly. Be nice. Do your best to remember the names of the people you meet. Because most offices are divided up into probate, dissolutions, juvenile, civil litigation, and so on, you should identify the person or persons who will be directly involved in the types of cases you do. For a clerk who has been doing his or her job for a decade or two, there is nothing more annoying and amusing than a know-it-all attorney straight out of law school. Instead of pretending you know everything, how about just admitting to them that you have a lot to learn and you would appreciate any help they could give you.

2. On subsequent visits to the courthouse, take some time to get to know the people who are working there. I am not suggesting that you interfere with their work, but if the opportunity for more casual conversation is there, find out about their families or their interests. You may be working with these folks for years to come, and it is truly enjoyable to get to know them on a different level.

3. Never—and I mean never—be rude. Do not be rude to the clerk. Do not be rude to the court attendant.

Do not be rude to the janitor. Their job is just as important and just as stressful as yours.

Treating court personnel as friends and colleagues will enrich your practice and your life in unexpected ways. My husband Pete, who is a former prosecutor, tells the story of being particularly discouraged about a case as he waited for a jury verdict. The court attendant noticed how bad Pete was feeling and made a special point to reach out to him and cheer him up. This small act of kindness made an impression on Pete, and he has never forgotten it. My wish for you is that you look for opportunities to show kindness to all those in the court system, and I guarantee that when you need some kindness yourself, someone will reach out and show it to you.

SECTION IX:

THE NEW LAWYER AT HOME

I love that movie where the little boy sees dead people everywhere. I felt a little like him after my first semester of law school except that I wasn't seeing dead people everywhere. I was seeing lawsuits everywhere. It was as if my professors had opened my eyes to all the dangerous breaches of duty that were looming everywhere. You will find, however, that people who haven't gone to law school don't look at the world the same way we do. As a consequence, living in a world of nonlawyers can be a challenge.

85.

DON'T CROSS-EXAMINE YOUR SPOUSE OR SIGNIFICANT OTHER

Being married is hard enough, and being married to a lawyer presents some even bigger challenges. Here are some common—and very valid—complaints from non-lawyer spouses:

- "He spends too much time on the telephone at home."

- "She works too many hours at the office."

- "When he's in trial, I hardly see him."

- "She's under so much stress that it makes her crabby."

- "I have no idea what he's talking about."

Add to that mixture that lawyers are more likely than the general population to suffer from depression and alcoholism, and the life of a nonlawyer spouse doesn't sound too appealing.

But there are lawyers out there who can conquer these complaints and have healthy, lifelong relationships. How do they do it?

1. *They don't cross examine their spouses.* So much of what you do as an attorney is second nature. When someone doesn't answer your question, you keep asking until you get the answer that you want. "Just answer yes or no!" may be okay directed at a defendant, but your spouse may be slightly put off.

2. *They limit or completely avoid the use of sarcasm.* Sarcasm is, quite simply, verbal aggression. It is a way to demean the other party and elevate yourself. It's not pretty. Many lawyers do it without even realizing it. So pay attention.

3. *They resist the temptation to insist on winning every argument.* "Winning" an argument doesn't promote the marriage or the relationship. You don't have to win. I read in a magazine that in every relationship each party should be able to say to the other, "Let's try it

your way," and really mean it. Not "Let's try it your way, and then I'll torment you when you're wrong."

4. *They don't keep score or harbor grudges.* The ability to forgive is essential. They know marriage is not always a fifty-fifty relationship. Sometimes it's ninety-ten. It's not always fun and you're not always happy. If you need some counseling, get it before your relationship has hit the crisis point. They know that the commitment they have made is worth fighting for.

You will put incredible time and effort into your legal career. Ask yourself, "Am I working as hard on my marriage as I work on my law practice?" That's probably the bottom line. If you show by word and deed that being a good husband, wife, or significant other is more important to you than being a lawyer, I think your relationship will be just fine.

86.

PHONE CALLS ON NIGHTS, WEEKENDS, AND HOLIDAYS

Many lawyers have the same fantasy. In this fantasy, they work an 8:00 to 5:00 assembly line job. They don't have to make decisions that impact someone else's life. They get scheduled breaks and a one hour lunch. At 5:00 p.m., they go home and spend their night focusing on family and engaging in activities they enjoy.

That's the fantasy. Here's the reality—the practice of law doesn't work that way. As much as you would love to have your clients experience their crises during normal business hours from Monday through Friday, life doesn't work that way. The attorney who practices criminal law may get calls from jail in the middle of the night. If you are a divorce attorney, Friday afternoons and holidays are prime times for visitation issues. If you are an employment law attorney, issues arise on weekends and also during the third shift.

So here are a few suggestions of how you and your family can manage the phone calls:

1. When a work call comes in, find somewhere to talk privately and jot down some notes if you can. This will also help you to remember to bill for the call.

2. Don't let the phone calls overtake your life. Turn off your phone during your daughter's softball game or your son's piano recital. With very few exceptions, waiting a few hours never hurt anyone.

3. Remind your client that the courthouse and the opposing counsel's law office are not open on weekends or holidays. Get your client calmed down, and let them know that there is limited legal action you can take outside of normal business hours.

Being available by phone allows me to get out of the office and have a more flexible schedule instead of being tied to my desk. When I'm out of the office, I never have to worry if something is happening in my cases, because if it is, someone will call me. Even so, time with your family is too important to spend it off in a corner talking with a client. So get your business done and get back to your family as quickly as you can.

87.

FIND A CREATIVE OUTLET AND A PHYSICAL OUTLET

Lawyers who have sacrificed everything for their law practices are unhappy. They don't have an identity. They don't have hobbies. They don't have healthy relationships. If you are expected to bill twenty-one-hundred hours per year, you don't feel employed, you feel owned. I have a friend who says, "Law firms are like cats. They don't love you, they are just using you." The message is clear—You cannot rely on your law practice or law firm to make you happy. That is up to you.

Because of the pressures that you constantly face as an attorney, I can't stress enough how important it is for you to insist on balance in your life. Balance is not the time you spend drinking after work. Balance involves both creative and physical outlets. Achieving and maintaining a healthy balance will actually energize your life.

How do you find the outlet that is right for you? Start by thinking back to when you were growing up. What made you happy? Was it riding your bike? Was it playing the piano? Was it painting a picture? What did you dream of doing? Maybe you dreamed of running a marathon or learning to tap dance. My suggestion? Do it! Maybe you dreamed of knitting a sweater or making a quilt. My suggestion? Do it! There is nothing stopping you except your own insecurity. Don't use the excuse that you don't have the time. You do have the time. And trust me, when you find something outside your law practice that affirms you and that you get satisfaction from, your law career will be not just tolerable—it may actually be enjoyable.

One final thought. Take an annual vacation. Get away from everything with your family and friends. Turn the Blackberry off, put your watch away, and breathe.

88.

GET YOUR AFFAIRS IN ORDER

Attorneys often procrastinate when it comes to putting their affairs in order. Consider this example: A probate attorney spent his entire career resolving will disputes in court. But when the probate attorney died, his law partner could not find his will. His assistant insisted that a will must exist because the attorney had said his affairs were in order. The law partner shook his head and said, "If you had been in the [practice of law] as long as I had, you would know that there is no subject on which men are so inconsistent and so little to be trusted."

This isn't a "ripped from the headlines" story. It is from *David Copperfield* by Charles Dickens. Because the book was published in 1850, it is safe to assume that attorneys have been struggling with this issue for quite some time.

Attorneys spend their lives taking care of other people's affairs, so why don't they take care of their own? Two reasons. One, it's the same reason teenagers drive too fast. They don't think anything bad will ever happen to them. Two, it's easier to look at someone else's life in a dispassionate light instead of turning that same light on your own affairs.

Quite simply, you need to have a will. You need to have a health care power of attorney. You need to have a power of attorney for your financial affairs. You need to have a safe deposit box to put them in. I encourage you to talk with an experienced colleague about what arrangements and documents may be in you and your family's best interests. If you are reluctant to do that, most state bar associations have standard forms that you can fill in yourself. Don't wait. Do it now. As one of my favorite senior judges used to say, "It's later than you think."

SECTION X:

YOUR LEGAL CAREER
IN THE LONG TERM

*It has often been said that your legal career is not a sprint,
it is a marathon. To make it to the finish line, you need to
stay curious, stay involved, and stay grateful.*

89.

KEEP UP WITH YOUR JURISDICTION'S LATEST ETHICS AND APPELLATE DECISIONS

I've taught Business Law at my alma mater for over a decade. Because we cover topics in one evening that a law school devotes an entire semester to, I brush with broad strokes. Although I cover the standard terms and concepts (i.e., what is a corporation), I try to teach my students another lesson, too. The lesson is that the law never stays the same. Even if I had the ability today to download every law directly into their brains, it still wouldn't be enough because the law may change tomorrow. So my goal—in addition to the terms and concepts—is to teach them to think a little more like lawyers and give them the tools to navigate the changing legal landscape that will most certainly occur during their business careers.

How can you stay current with the latest changes in the law and with the ethics and appellate decisions in your jurisdiction?

1. Read them at least every month. If you no longer get the updates via mail, go to your supreme court's website and read them there.

2. Read your state bar association's monthly magazine or newsletter from cover to cover. I guarantee that it will contain useful information that you will refer to again and again.

3. Attend well-organized, relevant, continuing legal education (CLE) seminars. The handouts you receive from the seminars will be the starting point for many research projects. A word of warning—Every jurisdiction has minimum requirements for attendance at CLEs each year. Don't wait until the last minute to get your hours. Accumulate as many as you can early in the year because life always finds a way to disrupt your plans. Finally, get your report filed on time. Your law license depends on it.

4. If you want to go a step further, find a class to teach at a local community college or university. The best way to master a subject is to figure out how you would explain it to someone else. There is no better way to learn something than to have to teach it.

90.

DON'T LET THE
DOOR HIT YOU

Many law firms should have a revolving door installed at their entrance. The letterhead is changing constantly. Lawyers come and lawyers go, and yet despite the frequency with which it happens, they still manage to do a poor job of it. Feelings are hurt. Accusations fly. Whether you have been asked to leave or are leaving voluntarily, there is a right and a wrong way to leave your firm.

The wrong way starts with you deciding to leave and then attempting to take coworkers and clients with you. You have a duty of loyalty to your firm, and your preparations to leave cannot involve anything that will damage it including making derogatory statements to clients. Some lawyers use their exit as an opportunity to wreak vengeance wherever and to whomever possible. They don't seem to understand that people will think they are a snake. These lawyers also seem to forget that serious ethical violations and even civil litigation can arise from this type of behavior.

Leaving the right way means that you are aware of and will follow the ethical and legal restrictions in your jurisdiction. It means that you have not lied to anyone about your intentions. It's okay to keep things close to the vest until your plans to leave are in place, but if someone asks you a direct question, you should answer honestly.

Leaving the right way also means that you don't wait too long to tell your firm. You don't want them to hear it from anyone but you. Even in the biggest city, the legal community is pretty small and word travels fast. You need to give your firm enough advance notice so that you can minimize the disruption that your departure creates for your clients and your office.

The bottom line is that you want to leave with your head held high. A gracious exit will be rewarded both in terms of your reputation in the legal community and also your relationships with former colleagues. If you leave the right way, people will be both happy for your new opportunity and sad to see you go.

91.

WHY LAWYERS GET BURNED OUT

It's hard for young, enthusiastic law school graduates to wrap their minds around *burnout*. It is no doubt an overused term. Maybe it's better to say "exhausted" or "grouchy." Or how about "dreams of opening a bed and breakfast"?

Many occupations are prone to burn out but the legal profession seems especially susceptible. Lawyers are under a lot of stress. Clients pay you a lot of money, and they expect results. There are deadlines. There are conflicts. There are fears of malpractice. But burnout is about more than just the job you do—it's about the person you are. Lawyers have personality traits that make it hard for them to leave their work at the office. Those traits are what give you a drive to succeed, but they also wake you up in the middle of the night after dreaming that a flood is here and the water is starting to come in through the windows.

Despite the work you do and despite your natural instincts, you can beat burnout. Your law firm may be able to help a little. Some firms are trying to make work life more enjoyable for their attorneys. They may give special little perks like pet insurance and valet dry cleaning service. But ultimately it is your responsibility to keep your own law practice in perspective. Remember that your practice doesn't have an ending date like the last day of school. Your practice is like a river. It just keeps rolling, and you have to roll with it. Your personal life is like that, too. In the words of the immortal Ferris Bueller, "Life moves pretty fast. If you don't stop and look around once in a while, you could miss it." Maybe the best definition for *burnout* should be "what happens when you stop looking around."

92.

YOU HAVE THE POWER TO PREDICT THE FUTURE (EVENTUALLY)

Some people believe that you never know what someone else will do and that there is no possible way for you to make an educated guess about human behavior. Those people are wrong. The longer you live, the more you realize that most people act and react to situations in a pretty similar way. I realize that your degree is in law, not psychology, but it will definitely help you to be familiar with both. It will help you with clients, opposing parties, and opposing counsel. If you know what is motivating someone, you can adapt your behavior and your arguments to get the best result for your client.

What can you do to predict the future? First, as you work with more cases and clients, watch for patterns. Pay attention to how people react in different situations. Think about what you can do make people feel more comfortable. Subscribe to a magazine about psychology. Befriend a therapist. When you are puzzled about why someone is behaving the way he or she is, ask the therapist. I am sure the therapist will be glad to enlighten you. Finally, turn the question on yourself when you are engaged in any behavior that could be described as even mildly self-destructive. When you have the maturity to ask yourself, "Why am I behaving the way I am?" your own life and your own future will make a lot more sense.

93.

STAY HUMBLE AND STAY GRATEFUL

Growing up, my brothers and sisters and I participated in a hundred different activities from softball to football to musicals to scholarship competitions. My dad's advice was the same regardless of what we were doing: "When you lose say little; when you win say even less." He taught us at an early age that complaining about losing and gloating about winning were a poor reflection on us and our parents. My parents' humility shaped all of us and how we viewed our place in the world.

Maybe that's why I'm bothered by attorneys who are convinced of their own superiority (which I actually view as a sign of their insecurity). Some of the most famous and beloved attorneys in history were known for their humility. Think of Abraham Lincoln and Mahatma Gandhi. Being humble is not a sign of weakness; rather, it is a sign of strength. Crowing and end-zone dancing after a jury verdict are not conducive to good working relationships among attorneys. There is such thing as a sore winner.

It's easier to stay humble when you stay grateful. I tell my husband that, regardless of the craziness that is happening in our lives, if the kids are healthy and we are all together, it's a good day. Don't let too much time go by without remembering how incredibly blessed you are. Don't waste one minute worrying about what you don't have. If your measure of success is accumulating what everyone else has, you will lead a joyless existence. Volunteering your time with those less fortunate than you is a great way to put your incredible good fortune into perspective.

94.

DO NOT UNDERESTIMATE THE POWER OF ADDICTION

Lawyers deal with addiction every day—with their clients, their criminal defendants, their colleagues, and their friends. Sometimes even with themselves. No one is immune.

I have a simple suggestion that I hope will open up a more meaningful way for you to understand addiction—Become friends with someone who is in recovery. My friend Ann is that person in my life. She has been sober for twenty years and still attends AA meetings once a week. I have learned more from her about addiction in the five years we've known each other than I had learned in a lifetime. The first book Ann recommended to me was the AA Big Book. The Big Book is a staple at AA and contains descriptions of the alcoholic mind, body, and behavior, and also personal stories of recovery. I am recommending this inspiring book to you, because I hope it will give you a new perspective on addiction. It may even help you to recognize the addictive tendencies in yourself and those around you.

An important lesson that I've learned from Ann is that you should never underestimate the power of addiction. Addiction makes people—your clients, your friends, your colleagues—do crazy, unhealthy things. Their desperation to hide their addiction leads to more secrets and more personal destruction. An addict will say anything they think you want to hear. They will look you in the eye and lie with startling ease. They will steal your money and then help you look for it. Enabling an addict doesn't help you or them. It just postpones the inevitable.

Once I asked Ann, "If you have not had a drop to drink for twenty years, why do you still need to go to AA?" Her answer was this: "Once an addict, always an addict. So while the desire is far less or nonexistent today, it's only because I go to meetings and keep that awareness about my addiction."

You don't have to be in recovery to use what they teach at AA. They give smart and helpful advice that applies to both alcoholics and non-alcoholics like, "Anger is a mask for fear and hurt." Think about it. The next time someone in your office gets angry, the correct question is not, "Why are they angry?" The correct question is, "Why are they feeling afraid or hurt?" When you approach it that way, you may actually help your colleague or your client get to the heart of their problem.

But I think the most helpful thing I've learned from Ann is this: Live in the now. Worrying about tomorrow is not going to solve the problems you have today. It will only distract you from what's important. Living in the now means dealing with today's problems today, and it also means counting your blessings today. Blessings, which I am fortunate to say, include very good friends.

95.

IT'S NOT THE CRIME—
IT'S THE COVER-UP

You are human. You will make mistakes. The people in your office will make mistakes. Everybody makes mistakes. The problems start to snowball when you try to lie your way out of a mistake instead of owning up to it.

Consider this scenario. You are working on a case with another attorney from your firm. He or she fails to do something. It may not be fatal to the case, but the mistake requires extra pleadings to be filed and extra time to be expended. Two months later at your annual evaluation, you find out that the other attorney went to the client and the managing partner behind your back and blamed you for what happened.

Unfortunately, the competitive atmosphere at some law firms will lead some people to believe that dishonesty is necessary to get ahead. It's not, so don't be lured into that trap. If you can't advance at your firm without being deceitful then you need to find a new firm.

Here is what happens when you lie:

- If you lie to your office and try to shift the blame to someone else, your coworkers will never trust you again.

- If you lie to a judge, your reputation will take a permanent hit.

- If you lie during an inquiry by the ethics commission, the punishment will be much worse than if you had simply admitted your mistake and requested leniency. The ethics opinions are full of examples of attorneys who are putting great effort into their deception. Have no doubt, you will be found out and punished.

Throughout your career, you will wake up in the middle of the night thinking about your cases. But if you are honest about your own behavior, you can at least rest easy about your integrity and your relationships with your coworkers.

96.

DOES IT PASS THE SMELL TEST?

Early in my career, I was having a discussion with a wonderful colleague about the questionable conduct of an attorney we knew. The attorney was insisting on staying in a case where it appeared he had a conflict of interest. The colleague I was discussing this situation with had served on our state's ethics commission for years and had seen a great deal of misconduct during his tenure. Here's what he said:

> *Attorneys who are in trouble want to dissect the Rules of Professional Responsibility both before and after they engage in the behavior at issue. But when you're practicing law the right way, you should rarely have to refer to the rules. You can ask yourself one question, "Does it pass the smell test?" If it has even the slightest odor, even if it is technically acceptable under the rules, you shouldn't do it.*

What a great lesson to learn as a young attorney. The rules aren't meant as the be-all-end-all of your obligation to your clients and fellow attorneys. They are the absolute minimum level of acceptable professionalism and competence.

You have worked hard and accomplished an amazing feat—you have been granted a license to practice law. Never forget that it is a privilege that is to be used wisely and never taken for granted. When you were given this privilege, you took an oath to uphold the law and follow the rules of your jurisdiction. You are an officer of the court. You are a living, breathing symbol of justice to the people around you. I encourage you to aspire to more than just the minimum level of acceptable behavior. In everything you do—both in and out of the courtroom and in and out of the law firm—strive to be a positive reflection on your profession and yourself.

97.

YOU HAVE THE ABILITY TO CHANGE PEOPLE'S PERCEPTIONS ABOUT LAWYERS

When I think of lawyers, I think of Atticus Finch from *To Kill a Mockingbird,* but the general public thinks of someone much less honorable. Every so often, people say to me, "You seem too nice to be an attorney." When my husband announced to his father that he was going to be a lawyer, his father quipped, "I guess that's okay if you don't want to work for a living."

If we want to change the public's view of attorneys, we need to reach out through community organizations. As an attorney, people will look to you as a community leader. Whether it's the hospital board, the church board, or organizing a community project, they will turn to the attorneys. These are the opportunities to contribute in a meaningful way and show our profession in a different light. It won't happen overnight, but if every attorney volunteered within their community, we would see a change in people's perception of us.

The public also views attorneys in a different light when we stand up for the principles that have made our country great. Whether it is letters to the editor in your local newspaper or speaking to groups both big and small, lawyers will earn the respect of the public when we defend the Constitution and fight for the rights of all people regardless of race, gender, age, ethnicity, or class.

98.

DONATE YOUR LEGAL SKILLS

Why do lawyers volunteer their legal skills to everyone from Legal Aid to the local domestic violence shelter? Do they do it to show how important lawyers are? No. Lawyers volunteer their legal skills to show how important those organizations are.

It's a refreshing change to volunteer your time. It usually is very nonconfrontational and doesn't involve contentious litigation. Your input results in positive growth for the organization, for your community, and for you. There are so many organizations that need help that you can find the one (or two or three) that interests you the most. Here are a few suggestions:

1. Your local domestic violence shelter. The federal and state funding for these safe havens are constantly on the chopping block. They can't afford to pay for even

the most routine legal services. Be available to them on an ongoing basis.

2. Sign up through Legal Aid to accept cases. Our court system should be available to all persons regardless of their economic status. If every lawyer took a case or two each year from Legal Aid, we would be making a statement as a profession that equal justice under the law is more than just a slogan—it's a right. These cases have the added benefit of getting young attorneys into court. If you are at a large law firm, these cases may be one of your only opportunities to see the inside of a courtroom.

3. Accept an appointment to your local Human Rights Commission or other organization that is monitoring discriminatory activities in your community.

4. Contact your local junior high and high school and inquire about their mock trial program. The students will show you true enthusiasm for the law.

5. Ask your church or synagogue if there is any way you can be of help. Whether it's title work or a contract negotiation, they will find something for you to do.

Serving others fills a hole in you that you might not even know you have. The discovery that you make is that even though you volunteer to show these organizations how important they are, the end result is that you get more than you ever give.

99.

THE IMPORTANCE OF DEFENDING THE INDEPENDENCE OF THE JUDICIARY

As attorneys, it's easy for us to get bogged down in and distracted by the facts of our cases and the business of practicing law. Problems arise when we fail to look up from our desks to confront the larger challenges that are confronting the legal community and our country. One such challenge is the assault on the independence of our nation's judiciary.

Whether it's criminal law or environmental law or any kind of law, what would happen if we turned the judiciary into a mere reflection of the will of the majority? What if judges felt the need to disregard the law and bow to public pressure? I submit that the result would be that the faith we have in our court system would be eroded, and people would no longer respect the work of the courts or their decisions.

For example, every day in courts across this nation, defense attorneys come into court asking judges to suppress evidence.

Everyone from the police to the prosecutor to the judge to the defendant him- or herself knows the defendant had the drugs or gave the confession. Yet the judge is asked to throw it out because someone violated the defendant's rights. If you would leave the judge's ruling to a popular vote, most people would prefer that the drug dealer go to prison instead of receiving a get-out-of-jail-free card. However tempting that may be, the Constitution applies to all of us—even drug dealers.

Attorneys have a special role in this process. We know from our education and experience that being the guardian of the Constitution is an inherently undemocratic position. Whenever we can, we should work toward and encourage a deeper public understanding of the role of the judiciary. A judge's job is to protect the rights of individuals against the will of the majority. We expect and justice demands a fair hearing and an open-minded judge. When politicians and others rail against "activist" judges, we should be the first group to rush to the defense of an independent judiciary. We need to educate people that "activist" judge accusations are the refuge of unsuccessful litigants. We need to say in no uncertain terms that protecting individual rights is important even when it's not popular.

The bedrock of our system of justice is the belief that our judges will uphold the Constitution and make their decisions without fear of retribution. When anyone vilifies the judiciary to advance their own agenda, attorneys should look up from their desks, stand together and say, "Stop."

100.

CARE ABOUT POLITICS

I organized my first political debate when I was in the fifth grade. I was passionate about the Ford-Dole ticket. My friend Linda was all about Carter and Mondale. Not too much has changed since then. I am still a total and complete political junkie. I love talking politics with people of any party. My children know the difference between delegates and super-delegates. My idea of a good time is watching *Meet the Press*.

I care about politics, but why should you? The first reason is very practical. We are lawyers. Lawyers work with the law. The law is made by politicians. Ill-conceived and poorly written laws make our lives much more difficult. So it just makes sense for lawyers to do what we can to ensure that smart, common-sense people are elected to public office.

Second, if you want to have an impact on the types of laws and policies that are proposed and implemented, you need to have an awareness of what is happening. It's not enough for you to rely on the lobbyist for the bar association to keep you informed. You need to do that for yourself. Read the newspaper. Go to see your elected officials when they are in your community. Be proactive about pending legislation that could impact you and your clients. The Internet gives you access to facts and information on every issue imaginable, so you really have no excuse to stand on the sidelines. Instead of complaining about the laws in your jurisdiction, take an active role in shaping them.

Third, you have been blessed with above-average intelligence and an amazing education. If you fail to participate, it sends the wrong message to your community. Set an example for the people around you by participating in our democracy.

101.

WHAT WILL PEOPLE SAY AT YOUR FUNERAL?

I was honored to attend the funeral of a local lawyer. He was a true gentleman in every sense of the word. As we waited for the service to begin, I read his obituary and realized I had no idea of all the accomplishments he had during his legal career. The reason I didn't know is that he didn't feel the need to talk about them. I am sure he appreciated the accolades, but they really had very little to do with how he lived his life.

When I saw him at the post office or at the courthouse, he always shook my hand and asked how my children were doing. He never talked about himself. His word was all you needed. He was loved by his family and friends. He was a leader in the community. He was a classy man through and through. His behavior was always a reminder to me that I could do better. His funeral was a tribute to a man who lived his life for others.

What will people say at your funeral? Will they memorialize you for that incredible Motion for Summary Judgment you filed in the Smith case? Will they remember you for always making your billable hours? Or will they thank you for the time you spent helping the domestic violence shelter or stocking the shelves at the local food bank? Will they admire that beautiful home that you worked so hard to buy, or will they remember how hard you worked to raise money for the new school?

You are a lawyer, but your career will not define you unless you allow it to. Instead of grand gestures, it is the decisions that we make every day that accumulate over time and have a lasting impact on those around us. It really is your choice about how you are remembered, so choose wisely.

CONCLUSION: WHY I LOVE PRACTICING LAW

When I was eleven years old, I told my mom that I wanted to be a lawyer. I never wavered from that goal. Fourteen years later, I had graduated from college and law school, passed the bar, and landed my first job. It was after my third child was born that I decided to stay home with my family full-time. For the next several years, I became an observer of the practice instead of a participant. I had time to give some reflection to what the practice of law was all about. When my kids were old enough, I could have done a variety of things but I chose to reenter my law practice.

Are you surprised that I made the choice to come back? After all, I've filled this book with tales of stress, burnout, and conflict. But I hope I've also filled this book with of tales of friendship, honest work, and a desire to help others.

Here's why I love practicing law:

- I love practicing law because of the gratifying feeling you get when someone you know turns to you for help with the full confidence in your ability to help them.

- I love practicing law because I love the legal community—the lawyers, the judges, the clerks in the courthouse, and the law enforcement officers.

- I love practicing law because it makes me feel useful, and I know that I am contributing to my community.

- I love practicing law when my clients tell me at the end of the case that they couldn't have made it without me.

- I love practicing law when my former clients care enough to send graduation announcements, birth announcements, and pictures of their children as they grow up.

- I love practicing law because of the intellectual challenge every day.

- I love practicing law because my children are learning about justice.

Your reasons for practicing law may be different than mine. Whatever they are, I hope that you will learn to embrace the challenges that are ahead and look at them as opportunities to develop a greater understanding of the law, a greater understanding of people, and a greater understanding of our place in our communities and in our society.

ABOUT THE AUTHOR

Karen Thalacker is an attorney in private practice and a lecturer in Public Law at Wartburg College in Waverly, Iowa. She is also an award-winning author of two knitting books for children.